Concise

General Knowledge

2019

Union Budget 2018-19 | 2017 At a Glance | General Awareness
Indian History | Geography | Indian Polity | Indian Economy
Science and Technology | Sports

Purushottam Kumar

CL MEDIA (P) LTD.

Edition : 2018

Typeset by : *CL Media DTP Unit*

Administrative and Production Offices

Published by : **CL Media (P) Ltd.**
A-41, Lower Ground Floor,
Espire Building,
Mohan Cooperative Industrial Area,
Main Mathura Road,
New Delhi - 110 044

Marketed by : **G.K. Publications (P) Ltd.**
A-41, Lower Ground Floor,
Espire Building,
Mohan Cooperative Industrial Area,
Main Mathura Road,
New Delhi - 110 044

For product information :

Visit ***www.gkpublications.com*** or email to ***gkp@gkpublications.com***

CONTENTS

UNION BUDGET 2018-19

UNION BUDGET 2018

Finance minister Arun Jaitley presented the Narendra Modi government's last full budget before the 2019 Lok Sabha elections.

KEY HIGHLIGHTS

ECONOMIC HEALTH

- Economy firmly on course to achieve high growth of 8%
- Manufacturing, services, and exports are back on good growth path
- GDP growth at 6.3% in the second quarter of 2017-18 signals turnaround of the economy
- Growth in the second half likely to remain between 7.2% to 7.5%

AGRICULTURE AND RURAL ECONOMY

- MSP for all unannounced Kharif crops increased to 150%
- Institutional credit for agri-sector increased to Rs.10 lakh crore in 2017-18
- Fisheries, aquaculture and animal husbandry corpus at Rs.10,000 crore
- New scheme Operation Greens with an outlay of Rs 500 Crore
- Govt to develop and upgrade existing 22,000 rural haats
- Agri-Market Infrastructure Fund with a corpus of Rs.2000 crore
- Allocation for Ministry of Food Processing doubled to Rs.1400 crore
- Loans to Self Help Groups (SHG) of women to increase to Rs.75,000 crore by March 2019.
- Increased allocation of National Rural Livelihood Mission to Rs 5750 crore
- Under Ujjwala Scheme distribution of free LPG connections will be given to 8 crore poor women
- Housing for All by 2022 - more than one crore houses to be built by 2019 in rural areas
- Plan for employment of 321 crore person days, 3.17 lakh kilometers of rural roads, 51 lakh new rural houses, 1.88 crore toilets, and 1.75 crore new household electric connections

EDUCATION, HEALTH, AND SOCIAL PROTECTION

- Estimated budgetary expenditure on health, education and social protection at Rs.1.38 lakh crore
- Ekalavya Model Residential School to be set up for tribal children
- Investments for research & infra in premier educational institutions at Rs.1 lakh crore in next 4 years
- Allocation on National Social Assistance Programme at Rs. 9975 crore
- World's largest government-funded health care programme titled National Health Protection Scheme announced
- NHPS to cover over 10 crore poor and vulnerable families (approximately 50 crore beneficiaries)
- NHPS to provide coverage up to 5 lakh rupees per family per year for hospitalization
- Rs 1200 crore for the National Health Policy, 2017 - additional Rs.600 crore for TB patients
- 24 new Government Medical Colleges and Hospitals
- Clean Ganga: Of 187 projects have been sanctioned, 47 complete
- Banks of Ganga declared open defecation free

MEDIUM, SMALL AND MICRO ENTERPRISES (MSMES) AND EMPLOYMENT

- Major thrust for Medium, Small and Micro Enterprises (MSMEs) – allocation at Rs. 3794 crore
- Target of Rs.3 lakh crore for lending under MUDRA Yojana 70 lakh formal jobs to be created this year
- Govt to make 12% contribution of new employees in the EPF for all the sectors for 3 years
- Outlay of Rs.7148 crore for the textile sector
- Increase budgetary allocation on infrastructure for at Rs.5.97 lakh crore
- To develop 10 prominent tourist sites into Iconic Tourism destinations
- 35000 kms road construction in Phase-I at an estimated cost of Rs.5,35,000 crore

RAILWAYS

- Railways Capital Expenditure pegged at Rs.1,48,528 crore

- 4000 kilometers of electrified railway network slated for commissioning
- Work on Eastern and Western, dedicated freight corridors
- Over 3600 km of track renewal targeted in current fiscal
- Redevelopment of 600 major railway stations
- Mumbai's local train network to have 90 kilometers of double line tracks at Rs.11,000 crore cost
- 150 km of additional suburban network planned for Mumbai
- Suburban network of 160 km at for Bengaluru metropolis

AIR TRANSPORT

- To expand airport capacity more than five times to handle a billion trips a year
- Regional connectivity - 56 unserved airports and 31 unserved helipads to be connected
- To establish unified authority for regulating all financial services

DIGITAL ECONOMY

- NITI Aayog to initiate a national program to direct efforts in artificial intelligence
- Department of Science & Technology to launch Mission on Cyber-Physical Systems
- Allocation doubled on Digital India programme to Rs 3073 crore
- To set up 5 lakh wifi hotspots to provide net-connectivity to five crore rural citizens
- Rs. 10000 crore for creation and augmentation of telecom infrastructure.

DISINVESTMENT & GOLD

- Disinvestment target of Rs.72,500 crore exceeded; expected receipts of Rs.1,00,000 crore
- New disinvestment target of Rs.80,000 crore for 2018-19
- National Insurance Co. Ltd., United India Assurance Co. Ltd. & Oriental India Insurance Co. Ltd. to be merged into a single entity
- Comprehensive Gold Policy to be formulated to develop gold as an asset class
- To establish a system of consumer-friendly and trade efficient system of regulated gold exchanges in the country
- Gold Monetization Scheme to be revamped to enable people to open a hassle-free Gold Deposit Account

EMOLUMENTS

- To revise emoluments to Rs.5 lakh for the President
- Rs 4 lakhs for the Vice President
- Rs.3.5 lakh per month to Governor
- Pay for Members of Parliament - law for automatic revision of emoluments every 5 years
- 150th Birth Anniversary of Mahatma Gandhi- Rs.150 crore for commemoration programme

FISCAL MANAGEMENT

- Budget Revised Estimates for Expenditure at Rs.21.57 lakh crore
- Revised Fiscal Deficit estimates at 3.5% of GDP
- To bring down Central Government's Debt to GDP ratio to 40%

TAXATION

CORPORATE / PERSONAL / CUSTOMS DUTY

- Growth of direct taxes in 2016-17 at 12.6 percent & for the financial year 2017-18 (up to 15th January 2018) at 18.7 percent
- Additional revenue collected from personal income tax totals Rs. 90,000 crore
- No. of Effective Tax Payers increased to 8.27 crore
- 100% deduction to companies registered as Farmer Producer Companies with an annual turnover up to Rs. 100 crore
- Real estate sector - no adjustment to be made for transactions in immovable property where Circle Rate value does not exceed 5% of the consideration
- Reduced Corporate Tax of 25 % extended to companies with turnover up to Rs. 250 crore
- No change in personal Income-Tax slabs
- Standard Deduction of Rs. 40,000 in place of the present exemption allowed for transport allowance and reimbursement of miscellaneous medical expenses
- Transport allowance at enhanced rate is proposed to be continued for differently abled persons
- Increase in education and health cess on personal income tax and corporation tax to 4 %
- More concessions for International Financial Services Centre (IFSC) to

promote trade

- IFSC concessions propose transfer of derivatives and certain securities by non-residents from capital gains tax, and non-corporate taxpayers operating in IFSC to be charged Alternate Minimum Tax (AMT) at concessional rate of 9 percent at par with Minimum Alternate Tax (MAT) applicable for corporate
- Payments exceeding Rs. 10,000 in cash made by trusts and institutions to be disallowed
- Long-Term Capital Gains (LTCG) to be rationalized
- Proposal to tax Long-Term Capital Gains exceeding Rs. 1 lakh at the rate of 10 percent, without allowing any indexation benefit - however, all gains up to 31st January 2018 to be grandfathered
- To introduce a tax on distributed income by equity-oriented mutual funds at the rate of 10%
- Customs Duty on mobile phones increased to 20%
- Customs Duty on certain parts of televisions increased to 15 %

RELIEF TO SENIOR CITIZENS

- Exemption of interest income on deposits with banks and post offices are proposed to be increased from Rs. 10,000 to Rs. 50,000
- TDS shall not be required to be deducted under section 194A
- Benefit will also be available for interest from all fixed deposit schemes and recurring deposit schemes
- Hike in deduction limit for health insurance premium and/ or medical expenditure from Rs. 30,000 to Rs. 50,000 under section 80D.
- Increase in deduction limit for medical expenditure increased to Rs. 1 lakh under section 80DDB

DO YOU KNOW THESE TRIVIA ABOUT THE BUDGET?

- Origin: from Old French bougette, diminutive of bouge 'leather bag', from Latin bulga 'leather bag, knapsack', of Gaulish origin.
- Compare with bulge. The word originally meant a pouch or wallet, and later its contents.
- In the mid 18th century, the Chancellor of the Exchequer, in presenting his annual statement, was said 'to open the budget'.

- The budget was first introduced in India on 7 April, 1860 by the East-India Company to the British Crown.
- The Union Budget of India, also referred to as the Annual financial statement in the Article 112 of the Constitution of India, is the annual budget of the Republic of India.
- The budget, which is presented by means of the Financial bill and the Appropriation bill has to be passed by the Houses before it can come into effect on April 1, the start of India's financial year.
- Shanmukham Chetty, first Finance Minister of India presented the budget in November 1947 without any tax proposals.
- Liaquat Ali Khan was the finance minister of the All India Muslim League from October 1946 to Independence in 1947.
- John Mathai was the third finance minister to present the budget in 1950-51 before C.D Deshmukh, who presented the budget in the newly formed Indian Parliament.

ECONOMIC SURVEY 2018:

INDIA WILL BECOME THE FASTEST ECONOMY, FY 19 ESTIMATES GDP 7 TO 7.5%

The Economic Survey, which sets the scene for Finance Minister Arun Jaitley's fifth annual budget, forecasts that the country's gross domestic product (GDP) will grow by 7 percent to 7.5 percent in 2018-19. The Economic Survey for 2017-18, presented in the Parliament by Finance Minister Arun Jaitley today, underlined the need for more reforms.

KEY HIGHLIGHTS

- GDP to grow 7-7.5% in FY19; India to regain fastest growing major economy tag
- GDP growth to be 6.75% in FY2017-18
- Policy vigilance required next fiscal if high oil prices persist or stock prices correct sharply
- Policy agenda for next year — support agriculture, privatise Air India, finish bank recapitalization
- GST data shows 50% rise in number of indirect taxpayers
- Tax collection by states, local governments significantly lower than those in other federal countries

- Demonetisation has encouraged financial savings
- Insolvency Code being actively used to resolve NPA woes
- Retail inflation averaged 3.3% in 2017-18, lowest in last 6 fiscals
- India needs to address pendency, delays and backlogs in the appellate and judicial arenas
- Urban migration leading to feminization of farm sector
- Rs 20,339 cr approved for interest subvention for farmers in current fiscal
- FDI in services sector rises 15% in 2017-18 on reforms
- Fiscal federalism, accountability to help avoid low equilibrium trap
- India's external sector to remain strong on likely improvement in global trade
- Technology should be used for better enforcement of labour laws
- Swachh Bharat initiative improved sanitation coverage in rural areas from 39% in 2014 to 76% in January 2018
- Priority to social infrastructure like education, health to promote inclusive growth
- Centre, states should enhance cooperation to deal with severe air pollution Suvey 2017-18 in pink colour to highlight gender issues
- Indian parents often continue to have children till they have the desired number of sons

■■

2017 AT A GLANCE

January

1st January:

- Mori, a tiny village under Sakhinetipalli mandal in East Godavari district of Andhra Pradesh, sealed its place on India's digital map by transforming completely into a Smart Digital Village, in every sense of the term.
- India has successfully test-fired its home-grown long range intercontinental surface-to-surface nuclear capable ballistic missile Agni-IV from the Abdul Kalam Wheeler Island off Odisha coast.
- Two new Hindi writers Shraddha and Ghyansham Kumar Devansh have been chosen for Bharatiya Jnanpith Navlekhan Award for the year 2016, the literary organisation announced.
- An Indian-origin Saudi-based entrepreneur Shaikh Rafik Mohammed, who hails from Kerala has been appointed Major General of Kyrgyzstan, a rare military position occupied by an Indian in the Central Asian country.
- Shankar Balasubramanian, an Indian-origin British professor of chemistry and DNA expert at Cambridge University, has received a Knighthood for his contribution to the field of science and medicine along with Olympic stars Andy Murray and Mo Farah among others by Queen Elizabeth II for their contributions in respective field's.
- Air Marshal Anil Khosla took over as Air Officer Commanding-in-Chief Eastern Air Command on 1 January 2017.
- Rio Olympian Sathish Sivalingam from Railways won the gold, for the sixth consecutive year, in the men's 77 kg category in the 69th men's and 32nd women's Senior National Weightlifting Championship, at the Ponjesly College of Engineering.

2nd January:

- Prime Minister Narendra Modi inaugurated the five-day annual Indian Science Congress at the Sri Venkateswara University.
- Chandrababu Naidu, Chief Minister of Andhra Pradesh has launched a new health scheme, Arogya Raksha Scheme Tummalapalli Kalakshetram in Vijayawada to provide the medical treatment to the people of the Above Poverty Line at Rs. 1200 premium per annum.
- The Senate Functional Committee on Human Rights unanimously approved the Hindu Marriages Bill on 2nd January 2017.

3rd January:

- Justice Jagdish Singh Khehar has been sworn-in as the 44th Chief Justice of India. President Pranab Mukherjee administered the oath of office and secrecy to Justice Khehar at a function in Rashtrapati Bhawan on 4 January 2017.
- The 13th edition of Nepal's five-day Chitwan Elephant Festival kicked off in Kathmandu with the participation of over 50 elephants.

- Finland has become the first country in the world to pay a basic income to randomly picked citizens on a national level in an aiming at dismissing poverty, motivate people to join work force and decrease unemployment.

4th January:

- The United Nations 70th General Assembly has recognised the year 2017 as the International Year of Sustainable Tourism for Development.
- Telangana and Assam signed memoranda of understanding (MoUs) to join the Ujwal Discom Assurance Yojna (UDAY) taking the total number of states covered under the scheme to 20.

5th January:

- Veteran actor Om Puri has passed away after a massive heart attack.The actor was 66.He has been awarded Padma Shri, the fourth highest civilian award of India.
- UK Senior diplomat Sir Tim Barrow was appointed the new ambassador to the European Union (EU).
- Vice President Hamid Ansari on 4 January 2017 released a book titled The People's President: Dr APJ Abdul Kalam.
- Renowned Sitar maestro Abdul Halim Jaffer Khan died due to cardiac arrest. Abdul Halim Jaffer Khan was an Indian sitar player and received the national awards Padma Shri (1970) and Padma Bhushan (2006) and was awarded the Sangeet Natak Akademi Award for 1987.

6th January:

- Japan has decided to be associated with the development of Chennai, Ahmedabad and Varanasi as smart cities. This was conveyed by Japan's Ambassador to India Mr.Kenji Hiramatsu during his meeting with Minister of Urban Development Shri M.Venkaiah Naidu.

8th January:

- Gujarat government has come up with India's first student startup and innovation policy, which aims to provide Rs 200 crore in the form of grants to ideas developed by them.

9th January:

- Maharashtra government has launched India's largest public WiFi service called 'MumbaiWifi'.
- The 74th Annual Golden Globe Awards ceremony was organized at Beverly Hills, California, United States (US). This year, *La La Land*, a romantic musical comedy-drama film won in all the seven categories including the top award of best musical or comedy. Veteran actress Meryl Streep was bestowed with the Cecil B. DeMille Lifetime Achievement Award.

10th January:

- Prime Minister Narendra Modi has inaugurated the 'The Nobel Prize' exhibition at Science City in Gandhinagar.
- To promote ease of ticketing through digital transactions, railway minister Suresh Prabhu released the new passenger mobile the application named 'IRCTC Rail Connect app'.
- Former wrestler and coach Mahavir Singh Phogat launched his authorized biography 'Akhada' in Chandigarh.

11th January:

- World Bank projected a global growth of 2.7% in 2017, even as it observed that stagnant global trade, subdued investment and heightened policy uncertainty marked another difficult year for the world economy.

12th January:

- 12 January of every year is observed as National Youth Day, the birthday of Swami Vivekananda a grateful nation is celebrating Swamiji's hundred fifty-fourth birth anniversary with much fanfare.
- Khanderi, the second Scorpene class submarine that has superior stealth and the ability to launch a crippling attack with torpedoes as well as tube-launched anti-ship missiles whilst underwater or on the surface, launched at the Mazagon Dock Shipbuilders Limited, Mumbai.
- Actress Tisca Chopra named as Best Actress for Chutney at the Jio Filmfare Short Film Awards.
- Norway has become the first country to cease FM radio broadcasting.

13th January:

- Ecuador has taken over from Thailand as chair of the Group of 77 which promotes the interests of the 134 developing countries it represents at the United Nations, including China.

14th January:

- Gujarat won their first ever Ranji Trophy title beating Mumbai by five wickets in the final at the Holkar stadium in Indore.

16th January:

- The new Adoption Regulations have come into force on 16 January 2017, which have replaced the Adoption Guidelines, 2015, will further strengthen the adoption program in the country by streamlining the process

17th January:

- Kozhikode Corporation was declared as the first Elderly-Friendly Corporation in Kerala.

18th January:

- Indian passport has been ranked a lowly 78 in a global ranking of the world's most powerful passports which was topped by Germany.
- The world's ultralight high-performance mechanical watch RM 50-03 was inaugurated on January 16, 2017 at the 27th edition of the Salon International De La Haute Horlogerie (SIHH) in Geneva.

19th January:

- India's IT Hub, Bengaluru has been ranked at the top position in the 2017 City.

20th January:

- RBI Governor Urjit Patel appeared before the Parliamentary Standing Committee on Finance and briefed the panel about government's recent decision to demonetize high value currency.
- The International Olympic Committee (IOC) and Chinese e-commerce firm Alibaba Group entered into a long-term partnership through 2028 at the World Economic Forum in Davos, Switzerland.

21st January:

- The largest warship of the Indian Navy, INS Vikramditya, will be equipped with its own dedicated ATM.
- Mr Donald Trump has taken over as the 45th President of the United States, he took over the reins from Barack Obama 20 January 2017

22nd January:

- India's ace shuttler Saina Nehwal has won the Malaysia Masters Grand Prix Gold title at Sarawak in Malaysia.

23rd January:

- Hong Kong has withdrawn the visa-on arrival facility for Indians travelling to Hong Kong effective from January 23, 2017.

24th January:

- Tamil Nadu assembly under the chairmanship of Chief Minister O Panneerselvam unanimously passed the Jallikattu Bill on January 23, 2017 to replace the ordinance issued on January 21, 2017 to allow the states traditional sport.
- Virat Kohli became the fastest batsman in the world to score 1,000 runs as captain in One-Day Internationals (ODIs) on January 22, 2017 in the third ODI against England at the Eden Gardens.

25th January:

- The Supreme Court gave the government nine months to replace the thrice-a-week dosage norm of tuberculosis drugs with a daily dosage regimen recently approved by the World Health Organisation to curb relapse and deaths during treatment.
- In United States, the Senate has confirmed Nikki Haley as the next Ambassador to the United Nations, making her the first Indian-American to serve on a Cabinet rank position in any presidential administration.

27th January:

- Havildar Hangpan Dada, who killed four terrorists before laying down his life in Kupwara on May 26 last year, has been awarded Ashok Chakra, the highest peace time gallantry award.
- A Keshav Krishna, a scientist at the National Geophysical Research Institute (NGRI) has been selected for the National Geoscience Award for 2016.

28th January:

- The government stated that 119 banks are connected with the Aadhaar-enabled payment system and 33.87 crore transactions have taken place through Aadhaar-enabled payment systems.
- Indian Space Research Organisation (ISRO) has successfully ground tested the Cryogenic Upper Stage engine meant for the rocket GSLV-Mark-III.

29th January:

- IndiaPost has become the third entity to receive a final license last week from the Reserve Bank to start its payment bank operations.

30th January:

- In a first, India's Fanattic Sports Museum opened to the public in Kolkata.

31st January:

- American President Donald Trump has signed an executive order to temporarily ban visas for refugees belonging to seven Muslim-majority countries namely Iraq, Iran, Libya, Somalia, Sudan, Syria, and Yemen.

February

1st February:

- The Ministry of Railway has proposed the Finance Ministry to create a non-lapsable safety fund named 'Rashtriya Rail Sanraksha Kosh' over five years with initial corpus of Rs. 20000 crore and contribute a portion to fund it in the Budget 2017 .

2nd February:

- Researchers have discovered microscopic sea animal Saccorhytus, the earliest known ancestor of humans along with a vast range of other species.

3rd February:

- India's Lakshya Sen has become the World No 1 Junior Badminton player. He achieved the distinction in the latest rankings of the Badminton World Federation (BWF). Fifteen-year-old is the first shuttler from Uttarakhand to attain the numerouno spot at the international level.
- India is expected to clock GDP growth of 7.1 per cent in 2017—18 as the country gets sufficiently remonetised and the schemes in the Budget play a supportive role, says an HSBC report.

5th February:

- England Test captain Alastair Cook has been honoured with Commander of the Most Excellent Order of the British Empire (CBE). He was awarded the CBE at the Buckingham Palace by Prince Charles.

6th February:

- Health Ministry launched Measles Rubella vaccination campaign in the country at a function in Bengaluru.
- Jharkhand Chief Minister Raghubar Das stated that state will give two per cent reservation to sports persons in government jobs and nutritious food to them.

7th February:

- The Union Human Resource Development Ministry led by under Prakash Javadekar is set to constitute a National Testing Agency (NTA) which will be responsible for conducting examinations for higher and secondary education.
- Alastair Cook has resigned as England Test captain after a record 59 matches in the role.
- Iran lifted up the ban it had imposed on United States Wrestlers, thus allowing them to participate in the Freestyle World Cup to be held in Iran in February 2017.

8th February:

- The Supreme Court has approved the government's plan to record the identification details of mobile subscribers through an e-KYC (Know Your Customer) mechanism linked to Aadhaar in a bid to enhance national security and prevent fake users.

9th February:

- Russia will miss August's World Athletics Championships in London after their doping ban was extended, the world governing body president Sebastien Coe said.

10th February:

- India's top-order batsman Cheteshwar Pujara added another feather to his cap on the first day of the Hyderabad Test at Rajiv Gandhi International Stadium against Bangladesh. During his knock of 83 runs, Pujara surpassed the 52-year long-standing record of former Indian cricketer Chandu Borde of highest first-class runs in a single cricketing season.
- Gujarat has become the first state in the country for establishing the cashless system in its public distribution system (PDS) of food grains. The beneficiaries who are eligible for subsidised food grains under the National Food Security Act (NFSA) will now need to carry only Aadhaar cards for getting their food grains in Gujarat.

11th February:

- The Minister of State (I/C) for Youth Affairs and Sports Shri Vijay Goyal launched the Mission XI Million, the biggest school sport outreach programme, in New Delhi in the presence of President of AIFF Shri Praful Patel.
- Folk singer from Punjab Satinder Sartaaj has been selected for the awareness project against human trafficking 'Blue Heart Campaign' by the United Nations Office on Drugs and Crime (UNODC).

12th February:

- The government recently appointed heads of 10 Indian Institutes of Management (IIMs), including the first woman to head one of the 20 premier B-schools in the country.
- The US and Japanese military have successfully tested the Standard Missile-3 (SM-3) Block IIA missile defence system by intercepting a medium-range ballistic missile target in space for the first time.
- The PSLV, in its 39th flight (PSLV-C37), will launch the 714kg Cartosat-2 series satellite for earth observation along with 103 co-passenger satellites, together weighing about 664kg at lift-off.

13th February:

- The centre has approved setting up the Electronic Development Fund Tele communication Ministerwith a total corpus of Rs. 6,831 crore to support entrepreneurship and innovation in electronics and IT.
- Former IFS officer Narinder Chauhan has been appointed as the next Ambassador of India to the Republic of the Philippines .
- The FIFA governing body has named Argentina's former soccer player Diego Maradona as the new Ambassador of the FIFA .The 56 year old will have major role in FIFA's activities to promote the game across the globe and will also be be involved in relevant development projects.

14th February:

- Indian Navy's survey class vessel INS Sarvekshak has become the first ship in India to be fitted with solar power system on board.
- Germany's former Foreign Minister, Frank-Walter Steinmeier has been elected as the new President of Germany. The 61-year old won by 931 votes out of 1,239 valid votes cast by the members of the Federal Assembly.

15th February:

- PSLV-C37 carrying CARTOSAT-2 series earth observation satellite and 103 nano satellites has lifted off from Sriharikota, Andhra Pradesh

17th February:

- India has been ranked 143 out of 186 economies in the annual Index of Economic Freedom 2017 released by top US based Think Tank, The Heritage Foundation. The Index measures the degree of economic freedom in the countries of the world.
- Bollywood megastar Shah Rukh Khan will soon host the Hindi version of popular international show TED Talks.

18th February:

- Melody Queen Lata Mangeshkar has been honoured with the 'Legendary Award ' 2017 by Brand Laureate. The Brand Laureate Awards recognise world-class achievement in branding amongst individuals and companies.

19th February:

- Odisha based National Aluminium Company Limited(NALCO) has signed Memorandum of Understanding (MoU) with The Energy and Resources Institute (TERI) in New Delhi.
- AirAsia became the first foreign airline to begin its operations from Srinagar international airport in Jammu and Kashmir.

20th February:

- Indian ace shuttler PV Sindhu achieved her career best Badminton World Federation (BWF) women's single ranking by being placed at 5th spot Previously the top seeded player was placed at sixth position.

21st February:

- Bharat QR code the world's first inter-operable payment acceptance solution, was launched as part of efforts to move towards less-cash economy at an insignificant cost, according to RBI.
- UNESCO celebrates International Mother Language Day (IMLD) on February 21, 2017 under the theme "Towards Sustainable Futures through Multilingual Education".

23rd February:

- The government has allowed women working in industries to take six months maternity leave pre-empting parliamentary approval on the maternity benefit amendment bill that is pending in the Lok Sabha.

24th February:

- Premier off-spinner Ravichandran Ashwin, broked Kapil Dev's Indian record of most Test wickets in a domestic season.
- The ninth BRICS Summit will be held in China's Xiamen city from September 3 to 5, 2017. The theme of this year's event is 'BRICS: Stronger Partnership for a Brighter Future'.

25th February:

- The government has roped in actress Shilpa Shetty as a brand ambassador for the Indian government's cleanliness initiative Swachh Bharat Mission.

27th February:

- The 89th Academy Awards ceremony (commonly referred as Oscar Awards) , presented by the Academy of Motion Picture Arts and Sciences (AMPAS) to honor the best films of 2016, in 24 categories, held at the Dolby Theater in Los Angeles, California.
- The world's first robot table tennis tutor FORPHEUS in Japan has set a new Guinness World Record for its uncanny ability of being able to play the game better than most humans.

28th February:

- Indian international cricketer Virat Kohli has named as the 'Captain of the Year' at the 10th annual ESPNcricinfo Awards.
- Afghanistan cricket broke a new barrier when Mohammad Nabi and Rashid Khan became the first from the war-torn nation to be picked in the Indian Premier League (IPL) auction.

March

1st March:

- The government has shifted the responsibility of promoting digital transactions in the country to the Ministry of IT and Electronics (MEITY) from NITI Aayog.

2nd March:

- India's Ballistic Missile Defence (BMD) shield got a further fillip with the successful test of an interceptor supersonic missile conducted by the Defence Research and Development Organisation (DRDO).
- Telecom Secretary J S Deepak was named India's next Ambassador to the World Trade Organisation (WTO) from June 2017.

3rd March:

- The Indian navy successfully test-fired an anti-ship missile for the first time from an indigenously built Kalvari class submarine.

4th March:

- Students will now be required to have an Aadhaar number for getting their midday meals across the country.
- The Ministry of Women & Child Development is observing the Swachhta Pakhwada from March 1, 2017 to March 15, 2017 to raise awareness about Swachh Bharat Abhiyan among women and children.

6th March:

- *INS Viraat*, the world's oldest aircraft carrier in active service will be decommissioned on 6 March 2017 with a ceremonial send-off in Mumbai.
- Telecom operator Bharti Airtel has signed an agreement with Millicom International Cellular to combine their operations in Ghana.
- Kerala has achieved the maximum number of registrations under the Goods and Services Tax (GST) regime with at least 60% of an estimated 2.5 lakh traders migrating to the new platform.

7th March:

- Mumbai-headquartered HDFC Bank has launched India's first artificial intelligence based banking chatbot Electronic Virtual Assistant (EVA) for customer services.

8th March:

- GMR group led Rajiv Gandhi Hyderabad International Airport has secured first position in the world in the prestigious Airports Council International (ACI) Airport Service Quality (ASQ) survey in the 5-15 million passengers per annum (MPPA) category for the year 2016.

9th March:

- Union Environment, Forest and Climate Change, Anil Madhav Dave, launched the web portal for obtaining Coastal Regulation Zone clearances in New Delhi.

11th March:

- A South African man Chris Bertish has become the first person to cross the Atlantic Ocean on a stand-up paddleboard after completing an epic 4,050-mile voyage alone at sea.

12th March:

- Dangal' won the Viewer's Choice Best Film award at Zee Cine Awards 2017 on 11th March 2017.
- Thai contestant Jiratchaya Sirimongkolnawin was crowned Miss International Queen 2016 on Friday at a contest billed as the world's largest and most popular transgender pageant.

13th March:

- Indian cricketing legend Sachin Tendulkar was announced as the official ambassador of Women's Cricket World Cup 2017 by the International Cricket Council (ICC) yesterday, on the occasion of International Women's Day.

16th March:

- Captain Amarinder Singh, who led the Congress to victory in Punjab after a decade, will be sworn-in as the Chief Minister for the second time.
- Union Minister of State for Heavy Industries and Public Enterprises, Babul Supriyo has been named as Vice President of the 2017 U-17 FIFA World Cup organizing committee.

17th March:

- India's most successful Badminton Doubles specialist Jwala Gutta has been appointed a member of the governing body of Sports Authority of India (SAI).

18th March:

- RBI has been authorized by Government of India (GOI) to conduct field trials of plastic notes of Rs 10 in five cities across the country viz Kochi, Mysore, Jaipur, Shimla and Bhubaneswar.

21st March:

- The Government has approved a new scheme to provide financial assistance or capital subsidy to small powerloom units, for installation of Solar Photo Voltaic (SPV) plant, in order to alleviate the problem of power cut and shortages faced by decentralized powerloom units in India.Under the Solar Energy Scheme, the plants have two options:

22nd March:

- In Cricket, Tamil Nadu has won the domestic 50-over competition, the Vijay Hazare Trophy, for the fifth time.

23rd March:

- The Rs 3-lakh limit proposed for cash payments in the Budget for 2017-18 will be brought down to Rs 2 lakh as part of an unprecedented 40 amendments to the Finance Bill. Finance Minister Arun Jaitley announced the amendments in the lower House.

24th March:

- The 8th Laadli Media Awards for Gender Sensitivity 2016 (Northern and Eastern Region) were announced at the Chinmaya Mission in New Delhi.

25th March:

- After making Aadhaar mandatory for filing income tax returns and applying for a Permanent Account Number (PAN), the government has moved to make Aadhaar-based e-KYC (know your customer) mandatory for mobile phone connections.
- Indian spinner Ravichandran Ashwin has broken the record for most wickets in a single Test season, taking his 79th this season during the Dharamsala Test against Australia.

26th March:

- Railways will set up Wi-Fi hotspot kiosks at about 500 stations and help people access an array of online services, including various government schemes.
- Pujara achieved the landmark for scoring the most runs in a Test season, surpassing the mark of 1269 by Gautam Gambhir which he achieved in the 2008/09 season.

28th March:

- Anushree Pareek became the first woman combat officer to be commissioned in the 51-year history of the BSF, the country's largest border guarding force.

30th March:

- Kerala, Tripura and Arunachal Pradesh have joined the Centre's power distribution company debt relief scheme, Ujjwal Discom Assurance Yojna (UDAY).

31st March:

- Sunaina Singh has been appointed as the new Vice-Chancellor of Nalanda University. She was Vice Chancellor of Hyderabad-based EFL University. She has replaced George Yeo.
- American astronaut Peggy Whitson made history when she floated outside the International Space Station (ISS)Indian forward player S V Sunil was named the Asian Hockey Federation (AHF) Player of the Year for 2016

April

1st April:

- Japan has committed an 'Official Development Assistance' (ODA) of 371.345 billion yen (about Rs 21,590 crore) under 2016-2017 for various infrastructure projects, including the dedicated freight corridor, in India.

2nd April:

- The BRICS-backed New Development Bank (NDB) has invested in seven projects totaling \$1.5 billion in about two years of its operation. NDB began operations in July 2015.

3rd April:

- The Government has launched PowerTex India, a comprehensive scheme for power loom sector development, simultaneously at over 45 locations in the country.
- Rajiv Kumar Chander has been appointed as the Ambassador and Permanent Representative of India to the United Nations Offices in Geneva.

4th April:

- A 1982 batch Indian Police Service (IPS) Geetha Johri has been appointed as the first woman Director General of Police (DGP) of Gujarat.

5th April:

- Haryana government has decided to provide a one-time grant of Rs 21,000 to all those families whose third girl child was born after August 24, 2015, under the 'Aapki Beti, Hamari Beti' scheme.

7th April:

- K Prithika Yashini, aged around 25 years, is the first transgender person to become a police official in India, appointed in Tamil Nadu.
- Rio Olympics silver medallist P V Sindhu jumped three places to achieve a career-best world number two ranking in the latest Badminton World Federation (BWF) rankings.

8th April:

- India and Bangladesh have signed 22 agreements in strategic sectors like defence and civil nuclear cooperation during Bangladesh Prime Minister Sheikh Hasina's visit to India.

9th April:

- Union Home Minister Rajnath Singh launched the website and app named 'Bharat Ke Veer', to facilitate the monetary contribution to the kin of soldier personnel killed in action.

11th April:

- The Survey General of India (SOI) completes 250 years.

12th April:

- Malala Yousafzai, the Nobel Prize laureate, becomes the youngest noble prize winner to address Canadian parliament.

14th April:

- Prime Minister Narendra Modi announced that women are free to retain their maiden names in their passports now after the marriage.

15th April:

- Uttar Pradesh government and the Centre have signed an MoU for the 'Power for All' scheme in the state.
- Former Governor of Jammu and Kashmir Girish Chandra Saxena has passed away at the age of 90.

17th April:

- Human Resource and Development Minister Prakash Javadekar launched the Rashtriya Uchchatar Shiksha Abhiyan (RUSA) portal and mobile app in New Delhi.

18th April:

- Prime Minister Narendra Modi inaugurated phase-I of the Link-II pipeline canal of the ambitious Saurashtra Narmada Avtaran Irrigation (SAUNI) Yojana in Botad district of Gujarat.

19th April:

- Tamil Nadu Chief Minister Edappadi K. Palaniswami dedicated the Indian Navy's indigenously designed 'P15A Guided Missile Destroyer', INS Chennai to the city Chennai.
- The Reserve Bank of India has set up two new Offices of the Banking Ombudsman for the State of Jammu and Kashmir (in Jammu) and Chhattisgarh (in Raipur).

20th April:

- Madhya Pradesh government has signed a power purchase agreement (PPA) with the Delhi Metro Rail Corporation (DMRC) to supply 24 per cent of electricity generated from the Rewa ultra mega solar project to be set up in the state.

21st April:

- Tata Power has signed an agreement with Ajmer Vidyut Vitran Nigam Ltd (AVVNL) for electricity distribution in Ajmer for 20 years.

22nd April:

- China successfully launched its first unmanned cargo spacecraft named Tianzhou 1.

23rd April:

- The National Health Mission (NHM) in Haryana launched a mobile-based application named 'Kilkari' to create awareness among pregnant women, parents and health workers on the importance of ante and post natal care.

24th April:

- Veteran actress Moushumi Chatterjee has received the lifetime achievement award, at the 80th Bengal Film Journalists' Association (BFJA) awards.

25th April:

- Belgium has become the first country to open an honorary consulate office in Gujarat International Finance Tec-City (GIFT City).

26th April:

- Internationally renowned sand artist Sudarsan Pattnaik from Odisha won the jury prize gold medal at the 10th Moscow Sand art Championship.

29th April:

- Union Health Minister JP Nadda has launched the Test and Treat policy for providing treatment to patients suffering from Human Immunodeficiency Virus (HIV).

May

1st May:

- Aymanam ward in the Kerala district on became India's first digitalised panchayat ward.
- Rafael Nadal won a record-extending 10th Barcelona Open title by defeating Dominic Thiem of Austria.
- Joshna Chinappa scripted history by becoming the first Indian to clinch the Asian Squash title

4th May:

- Swachh Survekshan 2017: Indore is the cleanest city while Gonda in Uttar Pradesh is the dirtiest.
- India to get world's highest railway bridge across Chenab river in J&K.

8th May:

- Justice Leila Seth: First Woman Chief Justice of a State High Court Passed Away

9th May:

- Great Britain wins Sultan Azlan Shah Cup hockey tournament.

12th May:

- The government has named Road Transport and Highways Secretary Sanjay Mitra as its new defence secretary in a top-level bureaucratic reshuffle.

13th May:

- Konkona bags Best Director and Best Actress awards at New York Indian Film Festival.

15th May:

- Sikkim Chief Minister Pawan Kumar Chamling was conferred with the first Bhairon Singh Shekhawat Lifetime Achievement Honour in Public Service by President Pranab Mukherjee.
- Assistant Professor in Department of Biomedical Engineering at Indian Institute of Technology – Hyderabad (IIT-H) Aravind Kumar Rengan has been awarded the prestigious Indian National Science Academy (INSA) medal in the Young Scientist category for 2017.

16th May:

- France's newly-elected President Emmanuel Macron has named Edouard Philippe as Prime Minister of France.

17th May:

- The USA based SpaceX has launched a communications satellite for Inmarsat, marking its first launch for the London-based mobile broadband company.

18th May:

- India's first Aquatic Rainbow Technology Park, an ultra modern exclusive facility for ornamental fish equipped with multi-species hatchery and live feed culture units, will become operational at Chennai.
- The US' National Aeronautics and Space Administration (NASA) will launch the world's smallest satellite named 'KalamSat'.

19th May:

- Turbo Megha Airways has become the first private airline to get a licence to fly under UDAN.

20th May:

- The Visakhapatnam railway station is the cleanest, followed by Secunderabad, among the 75 busiest stations in the country.

21st May:

- Arunachal Pradesh mountaineer Anshu Jamsenpa has become the world's first woman to scale Mt Everest twice in five days.

22nd May:

- India overtook Japan to become the second-largest steel producer in the world after China in 2016.

23rd May:

- Rohan Chakravarty, a wildlife and environment cartoonist from India, has won WWF International President's Award 2017.

24th May:

- Tedros Adhanom Ghebreyesus has been chosen to head the World Health Organisation (WHO).

29th May:

- The Manipur government has declared Dailong village of Tamenglong district as a Biodiversity Heritage Site of the state.

30th May:

- Satyabrata Rout gets Sangeet Natak Akademi Puraskar
- Love Raj Singh Dharmshaktu has become the first Indian to summit Mount Everest a record six times.

31st May:

- 43rd G7 Summit was held on 26-27 May, 2017 in Taormina, Sicily, Italy.
- India Development Report released by World Bank. India had one of the lowest female participation in the workforce, ranking 120th among 131 countries.
- Harmanpreet Kaur, the captain of India's T20 team has become the first Indian Women cricketer to play in Kia Super League, the England T20 League.

June

1st June:

- The 70th World Health Assembly was held recently in Geneva, Switzerland.

2nd June:

- In the above meeting member nations agreed to increase their assessed contributions by 3 percent.
- The first Mega Food Park in the state of Odisha MITS Mega Food Park Pvt. Ltd. at Rayagada.

3rd June:

- India has ranked 137th out of 163 countries on Global Peace Index 2017 published by The Institute of Economics and Peace.
- Odisha is the first State in India to have developed an automatic public address system that can be activated along its entire coast.

4th June:

- Varanasi will get the country's first 'freight village' spread over around 100 acres.
- West Indies cricket team's official name changed to WINDIES

5th June:

- India has successfully test-fired its first all weather tracked-chassis Quick Reaction Surface-to-Air Missile (QR-SAM).
- India has been ranked 45th, down four notches from last year, in terms of competitiveness in the annual rankings compiled by IMD which saw Hong Kong topping the list.

6th June:

- Telangana launches single-woman pension scheme, first in India.
- The book "The Ministry of Utmost Happiness" has been authored by Arundhati Roy, was released.

7th June:

- Nepal has signed a major deal with a China to develop a 1,200 MW Budhigandaki Hydroelectric Project.
- Veteran Nepalese politician Sher Bahadur Deuba was elected as Nepal's Prime Minister for the fourth time.
- Montenegro has officially joined North Atlantic Treaty Organization (NATO) and hence became the 29th member country of NATO.

9th June:

- Muttiah Muralidaran becomes first Sri Lankan to be inducted into ICC Hall of Fame.
- India, Pakistan Become Full Members Of Shanghai Cooperation Organisation.

10th June:

- President Pranab Mukherjee today launched the 'Selfie with Daughter' mobile application.

11th June:

- Thespian Bengali actor, Soumitra Chatterjee has been conferred with the France's highest civilian honour, the coveted *Legion of Honour*.
- NITI Aayog has launched SATH, a program providing 'Sustainable Action for Transforming Human Capital' with the State Governments.

12th June:

- Kolkata, the 'City of Joy' is about to experience a wonder in the form of an underwater Metro train which will run beneath the Hooghly river.
- Poet, essayist Haraprasad Das gets Kalinga Literary Award.

14th June:

- Uttar Pradesh tops the list with maximum child labor in the state.
- Group of Seven (G7) Environment Ministers Meeting was held in Bologna, Italy.

15th June:

- NASA confers Exceptional Public Service Medal to Michael A'Hearn posthumously.
- Leo Varadkar, a 38-year-old Indian-origin doctor, scripted history by becoming Ireland's youngest and the first openly gay Prime Minister of the Catholic-majority country.

16th June:

- Indian warships began a week-long naval exercise off the coast of Western Australia. The second AUSINDEX exercises are aimed at increasing interoperability between Australian and Indian naval forces.
- India continued to rise in the Global Innovation Index (GII) rankings for the second year in succession, after four consecutive years of decline. In 2017 rankings released in Geneva (Switzerland), India improved its position from 66 to 60.

17th June:

- Israeli author David Grossman has won the Man Booker International Prize 2017 for his novel 'A Horse Walks Into a Bar'.

19th June:

- India becomes 71st country to ratify UN International Convention on Road Transports.

20th June:

- The father of India's nuclear fusion reactor research program, Padma Shri Prof Predhiman Krishan Kaw, passed away.

21st June:

- Saudi Arabia's King Salman has appointed his son, Mohammed bin Salman, as heir, in a major reshuffle.
- UNICEF appoints Syrian refugee Muzoon Almellehan as Goodwill Ambassador.
- India re-nominates Justice Dalveer Bhandari for another term as ICJ judge.

22nd June:

- Indian agri microbiologist Shrihari Chandraghatgi given environment award in Japan.

23rd June:

- The Indian space agency ISRO today successfully launched its workhorse rocket PSLV carrying 'eye in the sky' Cartosat-2 series satellite and 30 nano satellites into orbit.

24th June:

- The West Bengal Government's Kanyashree Prakalpa was awarded the first prize in United Nations Public Service Award for Asia Pacific.

25th June:

- Manushi Chhillar from Haryana wins the title of Miss India 2017.

26th June:

- Indian shuttler Kidambi Srikanth has lifted the Australian Open Superseries trophy in Sydney.
- Venkaiah Naidu has launched the book titled 'The Emergency - Indian Democracy's Darkest Hour'.

27th June:

- The Aamir Khan starrer Dangal has become the first Indian movie to earn Rs2,000 crore worldwide.

28th June:

- Priyanka Chopra appointed as ambassador for Government's Skill India campaign.

29th June:

- India's communication satellite GSAT-17 successfully launched.
- Sharjah, a city in the United Arab Emirates was named 'World Book Capital for the year' 2019 by the Director-General of UNESCO, Irina Bokova.
- India's first blood bank for Cattle to come up in Odisha.

30th June:

- PM Modi inaugurates filling of Aji Dam at Rajkot by Narmada water.

July

1st July:

- Serbian lawmakers elected Ana Brnabic as prime minister making history by choosing both the conservative Balkan nation's first female prime minister and its first openly gay leader.

2nd July:

- India successfully test-fired its indigenously developed quick reaction surface-to-air short range missile from a test range along the Odisha coast.

3rd July:

- Achal Kumar Joti has been appointed as the next Chief Election Commissioner of india.

4th July:

- The Karnataka government has launched the 'Elevate 100' scheme to identify and nurture innovative start-ups.

5th July:

- New Israeli Crysanthumun flower named after PM Modi.

6th July:

- Pradeep Kumar Rawat appointed as the next Ambassador of India to Indonesia.

7th July:

- India is ranked a high 23rd out of 165 nations in a global index that measures the commitment of nations across the world to cybersecurity.
- Pakistan has successfully test-fired short-range surface-to-surface ballistic missile 'Nasr'.

8th July:

- Hamburg hosted the twelfth G20 Summit on the 7th and 8th of July, 2017.
- 122 countries approved the first-ever treaty to ban nuclear weapons at the UN meeting boycotted by all nuclear-armed nations.

9th July:

- Indian-origin man Guruswamy Jayraman awarded Australia's highest civilian award.

10th July:

- Ahmedabad city has been declared as a World Heritage City at the 41st session of UNESCO's world heritage committee being held at Krakow in Poland.

12th July:

- Mother Teresa's Blue-Bordered Sari declared an Intellectual Property.

14th July:

- A Model United Nations (MUN) Regional Conference is being held at Kathmandu.
- Rajasthan becomes the first state in the country to fix minimum educational qualification for contesting cooperative body polls.
- Gujarat to get India's first high-speed rail training centre at gandhinagar.

15th July:

- Raipur Airport Ranked First in Customer Satisfaction Index Survey.
- India is ranked 116 out of 157 nations on a global index that assesses the performance of countries towards achieving the ambitious sustainable development goals (SDGs)

16th July:

- The 18th edition of the International Indian Film Academy Awards was held in New York. Sonam Kapoor's film *Neerja* won the best film award. Actor Shahid Kapoor earned the Best Actor award for his role in *Udta Punjab*, while Alia Bhatt won the Best Actor (Female) award for the same film.

17th July:

- Justice Gopal Prasad Parajuli will be the new Chief Justice of Nepal.
- Roger Federer lifts a record 8th Wimbledon title beating Marin Cilic in Men's singles.
- I H Manudev has won the first National Masters snooker tournament title in Chennai.

18th July:

- TR Zeliang has been appointed as the Chief Minister of Nagaland.

19th July:

- Maharashtra government approved 'Majhi Kanya Bhagyashree' scheme, to improve girl child ratio.

22nd July:

- Ram Nath Kovind elected as India's 14th President polling 65.6% of the vote defeating the Opposition's joint candidate, former Lok Sabha Speaker Meira Kumar, who secured 34% of the vote.

25th July:

- Tax authorities of the five BRICS countries have signed a landmark document to establish a mechanism for taxation cooperation.

28th July:

- Dr. Harshvardhan launches "Sagar Vani" - An Integrated Information Dissemination System.

August

1st August:

- China formally opened its first overseas military base with a flag raising ceremony in Djibouti in the Horn of Africa.

2nd August:

- Dhrupad maestro Ustad Hussain Sayeeduddin Dagar passes away.

4th August:

- The Indian Army has developed a mobile application named 'Humraaz' through which serving soldiers can track details like postings and promotions.

5th August:

- Venkaiah Naidu is going to succeed Hamid Ansari as the new Vice-President of India. Venkaiah Naidu secured 516 and Gopalkrishna Gandhi 241 votes. This means, that Venkaiha Naidu will become the 13th Vice President of India.
- Veteran actress and national award winner Sharada has been selected for this year's Prem Nazir Award.

6th August:

- Mughalsarai to be renamed as Deen Dayal Upadhyay Railway Station.
- Akshay Kumar roped in as Brand Ambassador for Swachh Bharat Mission in Uttar Pradesh.

8th August:

- The Union government appointed Justice Dipak Misra as the next Chief Justice of India.
- India has celebrated the 75th anniversary of the Quit India Movement. This year's theme is "SANKALP SE SIDDHI"- the Attainment through Resolve.

9th August:

- India ranked 43rd position in 2017 Global Retirement Index (GRI).

11th August:

- Uttar Pradesh Government has launched a new awareness drive called *Namami Gange Jagriti Yatra*.

12th August:

- The Government of India has decided to launch a new sub-scheme named "Aajeevika Grameen Express Yojana (AGEY)" as part of the Deendayal Antyodaya Yojana – National Rural Livelihoods Mission (DAY-NRLM).

13th August:

- The 15th Ministerial Meeting of Bay of Bengal Initiative for Multi-Sectoral Technical and Economic Cooperation (BIMSTEC) concluded at Kathmandu, Nepal.

18th August:

- Pakistani rights activist Malala Yousafzai secured a place at Oxford University after getting her A-level results.

20th August:

- Telangana Chief Minister K Chandrashekhar Rao has been selected for the prestigious Agriculture Leadership Award-2017.

22nd August:

- Oinam Bembem Devi, the flagbearer of Indian women's football for over the past two decades was named the winner of the prestigious Arjuna Award.

24th August:

- Alibaba Group's Jack Ma is back on top as Asia's richest man following gains in the company's earnings and share price.

25th August:

- The Supreme Court of India pronounced that individual privacy is a fundamental right protected by the Constitution.

28th August:

- Justice Dipak Misra was sworn in as the 45th Chief Justice of India.

29th August:

- PV Sindhu won the Silver medal in World Badminton Championship 2017.

30th August:

- The Union Home Minister Shri Rajnath Singh inaugurated the YUVA – a skill development program. It is an initiative by Delhi Police under Pradhan Mantri Kaushal Vikas Yojana.

31st August:

- The Indian Space Research Organisation is all set to launch PSLV-C39 carrying Indian Regional Navigation Satellite System (IRNSS-1H).
- Gobindobhog rice, a speciality from Burdwan district of West Bengal, has got the geographical indication (GI) status.

September

1st September:

- India's largest autonomous public organization Council of Scientific and Industrial Research (CSIR) has been ranked ninth in the world.

2nd September:

- Prominent Konkani writer Mahabaleshwar Sail was presented with the Saraswati Samman 2016 for his novel 'Hawthan'.
- Former bureaucrat Sunil Arora was appointed Election Commissioner by the law Ministry.

3rd September:

- Economist Rajiv Kumar took over as the vice-chairman of government think tank NITI Aayog.

5th September:

- Ahmedabad formally accorded status of India's First World Heritage City by UNESCO.
- The 9th BRICS Summit was held from 3rd to 5th September in Xiamen, China. The Summit had five participating countries namely Brazil, Russia, India, China and South Africa.

6th September:

- The 12th edition of India-Nepal joint military exercise- *Surya Kiran XII* was held at Nepal Army Battle School (NABS) in Saljhandi, Nepal.

7th September:

- The Andhra Pradesh government has signed an MoU with the US-based Hyperloop Transportation Technologies (HTT)to build India's first Hyperloop system.

10th September:

- India has won 2nd South Asian Basketball, SABA, Under - 16 Championship. India defeated Bhutan by 131-50 in its last league match at Kathmandu in Nepal.

11th September:

- The renowned Indian Badminton legend Prakash Padukone has been selected for the first life time award by Badminton Association of India (BAI).
- The coastal city of Kochi is hosting the BWF World Senior Badminton Championships. The championship is been held in India for the first time.

12th September:

- Halimah Yacob was sworn-in as the 8th President of Singapore. She became the country's first female President and the first in five decades to come from the Malay ethnicity.

13th September:

- Shinzo Abe Gujarat Visit: India's First Bullet Train Project Inaugurated.

14th September:

- India has been placed at a low 103 rank, the lowest among BRICS economies, on the World Economic Forum's Global Human Capital Index. The list has been topped by Norway.

15th September:

- The book titled 'Unstoppable: My Life So Far' authored by tennis star Maria Sharapova was unveiled.

16th September:

- India's first Centre for Animal Law has been established at the city-based NALSAR University of Law in Hyderabad, Telangana.

17th September:

- Bollywood star Salman Khan received a Global Diversity Award at Britain's House of Commons.

18th September:

- Prime Minister Narendra Modi today launched the Sardar Sarovar Dam - the world's second-biggest - on the river Narmada in Gujarat.
- The 69th Annual Primetime Emmy Awards were announced at the Microsoft Theater, Los Angeles, California, U.S. *The Handmaid's Tale* became the first web television series to win the award for Outstanding Drama Series.
- Father of nephrology in India Dr KS Chugh dies of cancer at 85.

20th September:

- Akshay Kumar Appointed Uttarakhand Swachh Bharat Mission Brand Ambassador.

21st September:

- The Indian cricket board, BCCI has nominated Mahendra Singh Dhoni for the country's third highest civilian award - the Padma Bhushan, for his contribution to the game.

22nd September:

- The first of the Scorpene class submarines, *INS Kalvari*, was delivered to the Indian Navy by Mazagon Dock Shipbuilders Limited (MDL). The submarine will soon be commissioned into the Indian Navy.
- *Newton'* will be India's official entry for the Best Foreign Film category at the Oscars 2018, according to the Film Federation of India.

3rd September:

- Dr. Harshvardhan Launches Pt. Deen Dayal Upadhyay Vigyan Gram Sankul Pariyojana.

24th September:

- Prime Minister Narendra Modi has launched Sahaj Bijli Har Ghar Yojana or 'Saubhagya', to supply 24/7 electricity supply to poor households.
- Odisha Government launched 'Sampurna (Sishu Abond Matru Mrityuhara Purna Nirakaran Abhijan) Yojna' scheme for pregnant women in Odisha.

25th September:

- The Kandla Port, one of the top 12 major ports in the country, has been renamed as Deendayal Port in the name of Hindutva icon Pandit Deendayal Upadhyay.

26th September:

- Bilal Dar, a young boy from Srinagar has become the brand ambassador for Srinagar Municipal Corporation.

28th September:

- Madhya Pradesh has won the 'Best Tourism State' national award for the third consecutive year.
- *INS Tarasa*, a Water Jet Fast Attack Craft intended for extended coastal and offshore surveillance and patrolling, was commissioned into the Indian Navy.

30th September:

- Former Union Minister Satya Pal Malik has appointed as the new Governor of Bihar while Assam Governor Banwarilal Purohit will now be the new Governor of Tamil Nadu. Lt Governor of Andaman and Nicobar, Prof Jagdish Mukhi will replace Mr Purohit as the Governor of Assam. Admiral (Retd) Devendra Kumar Joshi will be the Lieutenant Governor of Andaman and Nicobar in place of Prof. Mukhi.

October

1st October:

- The Nobel Assembly at Karolinska Institutet has decided to award the 2017 Nobel Prize in Physiology or Medicine jointly to the American trio of Jeffrey C. Hall, Michael Rosbash and Michael W. Young for their discoveries of molecular mechanisms controlling the circadian rhythm. All three winners are from the US.

2nd October:

- The Meenakshi Sundareswarar Temple has been adjudged best 'Swachh Iconic Place' in India.
- The 2017 Nobel Physics Prize has been awarded "for decisive contributions to the LIGO detector and the observation of gravitational waves" to Rainer Weiss, Barry C. Barish and Kip S. Thorne of the Laser Interferometer Gravitational-wave Observatory.

3rd October:

- Mukhya Mantri Kaushal Samvardhan and Kaushalya Yojana flagged off in MP.
- Brenda Hale, First Female President of UK's Supreme Court.

4th October:

- The Royal Swedish Academy of Sciences has decided to award the Nobel Prize in Chemistry 2017 to Jacques Dubochet, Joachim Frank and Richard Henderson "for developing cryo-electron microscopy for the high-resolution structure determination of biomolecules in solution".

- The World Health Organization (WHO) appointed Soumya Swaminathan one of two Deputy Directors General. This is the first time such a post has been ever created within the organisation.

5th October:

- The Karnataka government launched the Rs. 302-crore Mathru Poorna scheme, aimed at providing free mid-day meals to pregnant and lactating women in rural areas.

6th October:

- Kazuo Ishiguro, "who, in novels of great emotional force, has uncovered the abyss beneath our illusory sense of connection with the world", has been awarded the 2017 Nobel Prize in Literature, the Swedish Academy announced.

7th October:

- The Norwegian Nobel Committee has decided to award the Nobel Peace Prize for 2017 to the International Campaign to Abolish Nuclear Weapons (ICAN) "for its work to draw attention to the catastrophic humanitarian consequences of any use of nuclear weapons and for its ground-breaking efforts to achieve a treaty-based prohibition of such weapons".
- Journalist-activist Gauri Lankesh, who was shot dead by unknown assailants recently, has been posthumously accorded with the prestigious Anna Politkovskaya Award, instituted by Reach All Women (RAW) in War.

8th October:

- President launches Mata Amritanandamayi Math Project Jeevamritham in Kerala.

9th October:

- The Sveriges Riksbank Prize in Economic Sciences in Memory of Alfred Nobel 2017 was awarded to Richard H. Thaler "for his contributions to behavioural economics".

10th October:

- Rajesh Nath, Managing Director of VDMA India, has been conferred the 'Cross of the Order of Merit', the highest civilian honour awarded to individuals for their services to Germany.

11th October:

- Actor Anupam Kher has been appointed the new chairman of Film and Television Institute of India (FTII), located in Pune. He succeeds former television actor Gajendra Chauhan.

12th October:

- Nisha Desai Biswal has been appointed as the President of the US-India Business Council (USIBC).

- Actor Anupam Kher has been appointed as the chairman of the Pune-based Film and Television Institute of India (FTII). He has replaced Gajendra Chauhan.

13th October:

- Union Cabinet has approved SANKALP & STRIVE Schemes to boost Skill India Mission.
- Union Cabinet has given its approval for signing of MoU by SEBI with Capital Markets Authority (CMA), Kuwait.
- Union Cabinet has given its approval for signing an MOU between India and Morocco on cooperation in the field of water resources.
- Dharmendra Pradhan has launched Prepaid Smart Card for CNG consumers.

14th October:

- John Flint has been appointed as the chief executive officer of HSBC Bank. He will replace Stuart Gulliver.
- Kiribati Republic became the 41st member to join the International Solar Alliance (ISA).
- Indian cricketer Yuvraj Singh has been named as the first Indian ambassador of the Laureus sports foundation.
- Ashish Nehra announced retirement from all forms of cricket.

15th October:

- Ajay Narayan Jha has been appointed as the expenditure secretary of India.
- Indian Air Force has launched an innovative mobile health Application named "MedWatch".

16th October:

- Union Bank of India launched an Android app named, 'Union Sahyog'.
- Veteran historian of medieval India and noted educational administrator, Satish Chandra passed away. He was 95.

17th October:

- Switzerland's Roger Federer defeated Spain's Rafael Nadal to win the Shanghai Masters tennis tournament title.
- Eminent poet, lyricist and journalist Prabha Varma has been selected for this year's Padma Prabha Puraskaram.

18th October:

- Bangladesh all-rounder Shakib Al Hasan became the fifth cricketer of the world to complete 5000 runs in ODI cricket and complete a unique double of 200 wickets.
- According to the NITI Aayog, the Gross domestic product (GDP) is likely to grow 6.9-7% this fiscal and while it is estimated to be at 7.5% in 2018-19.

19th October:

- Spain's Rafael Nadal defeated Nick Kyrgios of Australia to win the China Open 2017.
- Vijaya Bank has entered into MoU with HPCL for digital payments with BHIM application or UPI.
- The country's third largest private sector Bank, Axis Bank has acquired Freecharge.

21st October:

- Kavita Devi, a former weightlifter and South Asian Games gold medalist, has become the first-ever Indian woman to sign with the WWE.
- Actor Rajkummar Rao has been nominated in the 'Best Performance by an Actor' category at the 11th Asia Pacific Screen Awards (APSA) for his film 'Newton'.

22nd October:

- Ace gymnast Dipa Karmakar will be conferred with D Litt degree by the National Institute of Technology, Agartala, at its 10th convocation to be held next month.
- Indian golfer Gaganjeet Bhullar romped home to a three-shot victory at the Macao Open to bag his eighth Asian Tour title.

23rd October:

- The Telangana government will tie-up with a consortium of industries for setting up a rail coach factory in the state.
- Indian boxers won eight young medals including four gold in the third youth international championship Balakan Open in Sofia, Bulgaria.
- Badrikashram Jyotirpeeth Shankaracharya Swami Madhavashram ji Maharaj passed away. He was 76.
- Indian basketball player Amjyot Singh has entered the player draft for NBAs G League.

24th October:

- Prime Minister Narendra Modi launched India's first roll on-roll off or 'Ro-Ro' ferry service between Ghogha and Dahej.
- Additional director of the Central Bureau of Investigation (CBI), Rakesh Asthana will be the Special Director of this Chief Investigation Agency.
- India's star badminton player Kidambi Srikanth defeated South Korea's Lee Hyun IL in the Denmark Open final to his third Super Series Premier title.

25th October:

- State-run Numaligarh Refinery Ltd (NRL) has signed a 15-year agreement with Bangladesh Petroleum Corp (BPC) for export of diesel.

- Famous Malayalam film director I V Sasi died. He was 67.

26th October:

- Eminent classical singer and Padma Vibhushan awardee Girija Devi died. She was 88.

27th October:

- India's Jitu Rai and Heena Sidhu won gold in the 10m air pistol mixed team event at the ISSF shooting World Cup Final.

28th October:

- Tamil Nadu Chief Minister K Palaniswami laid the foundation stone for the aerospace park in Kancheepuram district.

29th October:

- Gutkha baron and Chairman of Manikchand Group Rasiklal Manikchand Dhariwal passed away. He was 78 years old.

30th October:

- India's young table tennis player Diya Chitale won the silver medal in the girls doubles category of the 2017 ITTF World Cadet Challenge.
- Indian junior men's hockey team defeated hosts Malaysia by 4-0 to finish third in the Sultan Johar Cup.

31st October:

- India's star shutter Kidambi Srikanth won the French Open Super Series Badminton Tournament men's singles title. This is his fourth Super Series title.

November

1st November:

- India signed a USD 200 million loan agreement with World Bank to facilitate investment in the agricultural sector and increase productivity in Assam.

3rd November:

- Assam government signed memorandum of understanding (MoUs) and Terms of Reference (ToR) with Singapore for skilling youth of the state.
- Noted Malayalam Poet and literary critic, K Satchidanandan, has been selected for this year's Ezhuthachan Puraskaram, Kerala government's highest literary honour.
- Energy Efficiency Services Limited (EESL), under Ministry of Power, launched a $454 million 'Creating and Sustaining Markets for Energy Efficiency' project in partnership with the Global Environment Facility (GEF).
- Olympic bronze-medalist Gagan Narang won a silver medal in the men's 50m rifle prone event of the Commonwealth Shooting Championships.

4th November:

- Noted Hindi writer, Krishna Sobti

will be awarded with the Jnanpith Award for the year 2017, country's highest award in the field of literature.

- Kenneth Juster will be the new US ambassador to India. He will replace Richard Verma as the top American diplomat in India.

5th November:

- Shuttler Kidambi Srikanth has reached a career-best world number two rank in the World Badminton Federation Men's Singles Rankings, after becoming the first Indian to win four Superseries titles in a year.

6th November:

- Shamika Ravi would be appointed as part-time member of the Economic Advisory Council to the Prime Minister (EAC-PM).

7th November:

- According to World Bank, India will be high middle income economy by 2047.
- MC Mary Kom has been named as the ambassador of AIBA Women's Youth World Championships.
- India has won the 2017 women's Asia Cup hockey title by defeating China.

8th November:

- Veteran actor Mohan Joshi has been Honoured with the prestigious Vishnudas Bhave award.
- India has baged 20 medals including 6 gold in Commonwealth Shooting Championship.

9th November:

- India Signed Loan Agreement with World Bank for US$ 119 Million for "Odisha Higher Education Programme for Excellence and Equity (OHEPEE) Project.
- An Indian-American, Ravinder Bhalla became the first-ever Sikh mayor of US' New Jersey-based Hoboken city.

10th November:

- Saina Nehwal defeated PV Sindhu Senior to win National Badminton Championship women's single title.

11th November:

- Eminent classical singer late Girija Devi will be honoured with the prestigious Sumitra Charat Ram Award for Lifetime Achievement for her contribution to the music.
- Legendary opener Virender Sehwag and former Delhi player Vinay Lamba have been made members of the Anti-Doping Appeal Panel (ADAP) of the NADA.

12th November:

- UNESCO member states appointed former French Culture Minister Audrey Azoulay as the new Director-General of UNESCO. She will the 11th Director-General of UNESCO and the second woman to occupy the position.

13th November:

- Ace Indian cueist Pankaj Advani clinched his 17th world title after defeating Mike Russell of England in the IBSF World Billiards Championship.

14th November:

- For the first time, the nation's financial capital will host the 34th annual conference of the Asian Bankers Association (ABA).
- Indian women's cricket team captain Mithali Raj bagged the Indian Sportswoman of the Year (Team Sports) award at the Indian Sports Honours (ISH) event held in Mumbai.

15th November:

- Pakistan's spinner Saeed Ajmal announced his retirement from all forms of cricket.

16th November:

- Bollywood superstar Amitabh Bachchan will be honoured with 'personality of the year award' at the International Film Festival of India (IFFI) in Goa.
- Super 30 Founder Anand Kumar has been awarded with the Rashtriya Bal Kalyan Award for the year 2017 by President Ram Nath Kovind. Anand has been awarded for his contributions in the field of teaching and education.

17th November:

- Minister of State (IC) for Power and New & Renewable Energy, R.K. Singh launched the Pradhan Mantri Sahaj Bijli Har Ghar Yojana – 'Saubhagya' Web Portal.
- The 15th Asia Pacific Computer Emergency Response Team (APCERT) Conference was held in New Delhi. It was the first ever conference to be held in India and South Asia.

19th November:

- RBI Governor Urjit Patel has been appointed to the Financial Stability Institute Advisory Board (FSAB) or Bank of International Settlement (BIS).
- Nicaraguan author and former politician Sergio Ramirez Mercado has won the 2017 Cervantes Prize. It is the Spanish-speaking world's highest literary honor.

20th November:

- Swedish telecom gear maker Ericsson has partnered with Bharti Airtel for 5G technology for the telecom giant's India operations.
- Reliance General Insurance Company Ltd has signed a comprehensive Bancassurance

agreement with YES Bank to distribute its various products.

21st November:

- Veteran journalist and mountaineer, Manik Banerjee has been awarded with the Life Time Achievement Award by the Indian Mountaineering Foundation (IMF)
- Former Wimbledon champion Jana Novotna died. He was 49. Novotna defeated France's Nathalie Tauziat in the final to win the Wimbledon title in 1998.

22nd November:

- India's Dalveer Bhandari has been re-elected to the International Court of Justice (ICJ).
- Acclaimed South African Indian-origin AIDS researcher Professor Quarraisha Abdool Karim has been appointed as a UNAIDS Special Ambassador for Adolescents and HIV.

23rd November:

- India has successfully test-fired the supersonic BrahMos supersonic cruise missile from Indian Navy's Sukhoi-30 MKI fighter aircraft for the first time.
- Bengali writer Nabaneeta Dev Sen has been awarded with the big little book award 2017 for her contribution to the children literature in Bengali Language.

24th November:

- Bareilly's Shubhangi Swaroop became the first-ever female pilot to be inducted into the Indian Navy.
- Former national rugby captain Aga Hussain has been elected the president of Asia Rugby. He has thus become the first Indian to occupy the post.
- Basel will become the first city to jointly host the Badminton and Para Badminton World Championships after it was awarded the 2019 edition of the Para event.

25th November:

- Assam's prominent film actor Biju Phukan passed away. He was 70.
- The Indian football team has been ranked 105th in the latest FIFA rankings.

26th November:

- India has won 10 Medals in the BWF Para-Badminton World Championships held in Ulsan, South Korea

27th November:

- Pankaj Advani has won 18th International Title Of 15- frame IBSF World Snooker Championship in Doha by defeating Amir Sarkhosh of Iran.

28th November:

- Indian shuttlers Srikanth Kidambi and PV Sindhu were honoured with sportsman and sportswoman of the year in Indian Sports Honours 2017 held in Mumbai.

- Former Expenditure and Revenue Secretary NK Singh appointed as chairperson of the Fifteenth Finance Commission. His tenure will be until October 30, 2019.

30th November:

- Senior IAS officer Ajay Kumar was appointed as the new Secretary, Defence Production, in the Defence Ministry. He has been appointed to the post with effect from December 1.

December

2nd December:

- Indian archers produced an impressive performance, grabbing three gold, four silver and two bronze medals at the Asian Championships.

5th December:

- Telangana Government will set up the World's first Information and Technology (IT) Campus for differently-abled persons (divyangs) in Hyderabad.

6th December:

- British singer-songwriter Ellie Goulding has been appointed as a Global Goodwill Ambassador for UN Environment.
- Melbourne will host the Golf World Cup for the third consecutive time in 2018.
- Uttar Pradesh's Shamli District has been included in the (NCR) National Capital Region.

7th December:

- India successfully test-fired 'Akash', its supersonic surface-to-air missile with indigenous radio frequency seeker from a test range in Odisha.
- India defeated Nepal by 3-0 to win the first ever South Asian Regional Badminton Tournament (team championship).

8th December:

- According to a survey conducted by online travel portal TripAdvisor, Taj Mahal is the second best UNESCO world heritage site in the world.
- "Dangal" was unanimously chosen the Best Asian Film at the seventh Australian Academy of Cinema and Television Arts (AACTA) Awards.
- Noted classical singer Pandit Ulhas Kashalkar will be awarded with this year's Tansen Samman given by the Madhya Pradesh government in the field of Hindustani classical music.

9th December:

- Portuguese star footballer Cristiano Ronaldo equaled the record of Lionel Messi to win the fifth Ballon d'Or award for the year's best player.

- India's Kumbh Mela has been recognised by UNESCO as an "intangible cultural heritage of humanity".
- Legendary Hindi writer Mamta Kalia will be awarded with the prestigious Vyas Samman 2017 for her novel 'Dukkham Sukkham'.
- Arun Lakhani, Chairman and Managing Director of Vishvaraj Group has been awarded the 'Most Promising Business Leader of Asia' award 2017.

10th December:

- Sri Lanka formally handed over the strategic southern port of Hambantota to China on a 99- year lease.

12th December:

- Priyanka Chopra has been honored with the Mother Teresa Memorial Award for Social Justice, for her work in helping refugees with food, shelter, and education.

13th December:

- Indian film "The School Bag" has bagged the Best Short Film award at the Vancouver Golden Panda International Film Festival.
- The Vice President of India, Shri M. Venkaiah Naidu conferred 'Yeraringan' Award to Prof. M.S. Swaminathan, in Chennai.

14th December:

- Indian golfer Shubhankar Sharma has won his first title on the European Tour.
- According to United Nation's Report, India's GDP growth Rate is projected to 7.2 per cent in 2018 and 7.4 per cent in 2019.

15th December:

- Rohit Sharma became the first batsman to score three double tons in One Day Internationals. He also became the first captain to score a double ton in the history of cricket.
- Harry Potter author JK Rowling has been named a 'Companion of Honor' by the UK royals.
- All India Council of Human Rights Liberties and Social Justice (AHILS) has awarded Swami Chidanand Saraswati, the President of Rishikesh based Parmarth Niketan, with the 'Global Peace Award'.

16th December:

- Prime Minister Narendra Modi commissioned the scorpene-class submarine INS Kalvari into the Indian Navy.

17th December:

- The eighth edition of 'EKUVERIN', the Indo-Maldives joint military exercise started in Belagavi, Karnataka.

- Switzerland's tennis player, Roger Federer has won the BBC Sports Personality of the Year Award for the fourth time.

20th December:

- Actor Sonu Sood has been awarded with the Punjab Ratan award for his contribution to the welfare of people of Punjab, specially his hometown, Moga.

21st December:

- Niti Aayog has planned to set up a Methanol Economy Fund worth Rs 5,000 crore to promote production and use of the clean fuel.

22nd December:

- The Union Cabinet has approved a project to set up India's National Rail and Transport University (NRTU) in Vadodara in Gujarat.

23rd December:

- Indian Army's Southern Command has conducted an exercise called 'Hamesha Vijayee' in Rajasthan.
- Lionel Messi, the star forward of Barcelona, has received La Liga's top scorer and best player awards for the 2016-2017 football season.

24th December:

- Jairam Thakur will be the new Chief Minister of Himachal Pradesh.

25th December:

- First-ever Air Conditioned local train in Mumbai flagged off from Borivali station.
- Manoj Sinha has launched DARPAN – "Digital Advancement of Rural Post Office for A New India" Project.
- Bengaluru has become the first Indian city to have its own logo.

26th December:

- Vijay Roopani sworn in as the Chief Minister of Gujarat.
- Uttar Pradesh Government has launched a free household power connection scheme 'Prakash hai to vikas hai' for the poor in the state.
- Dr Jitendra Singh launched an electronic-Human Resource Management System (e-HRMS).

28th December:

- Actress Anushka Sharma has been named Person of the Year by animal rights organisation "People for the Ethical Treatment of Animals (PETA)".
- India successfully test-fired its indigenously developed Advanced Air Defence (AAD) supersonic interceptor missile.

29th December:

- Small Industries Development Bank of India (SIDBI) has launched the 'Udyami Mitra' Portal (www.udyamimitra.in) to improve the accessibility of credit and handholding services to Micro, Small and Medium Enterprises.

30th December:

- Singer K S Chitra has been selected for 2017 'Harivarasanam' award, awarded by the Kerala government.
- Cholamandalam MS General Insurance has bagged the Golden Peacock award for risk management for the year 2017.
- Viswanathan Anand defeated Russia's Vladimir Fedoseev to win the World Rapid Chess Championship title Riyadh, Saudi Arabia.

31st December:

- Former Footballer George Weah has been elected as Liberia's president.
- The 105th Indian Science Congress will be held at Manipur University in Imphal, Manipur in March 2018.

■■

GENERAL AWARENESS

IMPORTANT DATES

NATIONAL

Jan 1	Army Medical Corps Establishment Day
Jan 8	African National Congress Foundation Day
Jan 12	National Youth Day (Birthday of Swami Vivekanand)
Jan 15	Army Day
Jan 23	Netaji Subhash Chandra Bose's birth anniversary
Jan 26	Republic Day
Jan 28	Lala Lajpat Rai (Birth anniversary)
Feb 2	National Day of Srilanka
Feb 5	Kashmir Day (Organised by Pakistan)
Feb 13	Sarojini Naidu's Birth Anniversary
Feb 24	Central Excise Day
Feb 28	National Science Day
Mar 3	National Defence Day
Mar 4	National Security Day
Mar 12	Mauritius Day; Central Industrial Security Force Day
Mar 16	National Vaccination Day
Mar 26	Bangladesh Liberation Day
April 1	Orissa Day
April 5	National Maritime Day
April 14	B.R. Ambedkar Rememberance Day; Fire Extinguishing Day
May 11	National Technology Day
May 24	Commonwealth Day
July 1	Doctor's Day
July 26	Kargil Victory Day
Aug 9	Quit India Movement Day
Aug 15	India's Independence Day
Aug 20	Sadbhavna Divas
Aug 29	Sports Day (Dhyanchand's birthday)
Sept 5	Teacher's Day
Sept 7	Forgiveness Day
Sept 25	Social Justice Day
Oct2	Gandhi Jayanti
Oct 8	Indian Airforce Day
Oct 20	National Solidarity Day
Nov 9	Pravasiya Bharatiya Divas / Legal Services Day
Nov 10	Transport Day
Nov 17	Guru Nanak Dev's Birth Anniversary
Nov 30	Flag Day
Nov 26	Law Day
Dec 4	Navy Day
Dec 7	Armed Forces Flag Day
Dec 10	Human Rights Day
Dec 14	National Energy Conservation Day
Dec 19	Goa's Liberation Day
Dec 23	Kisan Divas (Farmer's day)

INTERNATIONAL

Jan 10	World Laughter Day
Jan 25	International Customs Duty Day, India Tourism Day
Jan 30	(Martyr's day) Mahatma Gandhi's Martyrdom Day; World Leprosy Eradication Day
Feb 14	St. Valentine's Day
Mar 8	International Women's Day
Mar 15	World Consumer Day
Mar 19	World Disabled Day
Mar 21	World Forestry Day
Mar 22	World Day for Water
Mar 23	World Meterological Day

Mar 24	World TB Day
April 7	World Health Day
April 18	World Heritage Day
April 22	World Earth Day
April 23	World Books Day
May 1	International Labour Day (May Day)
May 3	International Energy Day
May 8	International Red Cross Day
May 15	International Family Day
May 17	World Telecom Day
May 31	World No Tobacco Day
June 5	World Environment Day
July 4	American Independence Day
July 11	World Population Day
Aug 12	International Youth Day
Aug 14	Pakistan's Independence Day
Aug 19	World Photography Day
Sept 8	International Literacy Day
Sept 14	Hindi Day, World First Aid Day
Sept 16	World Ozone Day
Sept 27	World Tourism Day
Oct 3	World Nature Day
Oct 4	World Animal Day
Oct 5	World Habitat Day; World Teacher's Day
Oct 6	World Wildlife Day
Oct 9	World Postal Day
Oct 10	World Mental Health Day; National Post Day
Oct 17	International Poverty Eradication Day
Oct 24	United Nations Day
Nov 7	Infant Protection Day; World Cancer Awareness Day
Nov 14	Children's Day/World Diabetics day
Dec 1	World AIDS Day
Dec 11	UNICEF Day

FIRST IN THE WORLD

The first person to reach Mount Everest	Sherpa Tenzing, Edmund Hillary
The first person to reach North Pole	Robert Peary
The first person to reach South Pole	Amundsen
The first religion of the world	Hinduism
The first country to print book	China
The first country to issue paper currency	China
The first country to commence competitive examination in civil services	China
The first President of the U.S.A.	George Washington
The first Prime Minister of Britain	Robert Walpole
The first Governor General of the United Nations	Trigveli (Norway)

The first Governor General of the United Nations	Trigveli (Norway)
The first country to win football World cup	Uruguay
The first country to prepare a constitution	U.S.A.
The first Governor General of Pakistan	Mohd. Ali Jinnah
The first country to host NAM summit	Belgrade (Yugoslavia)
The first European to attack India	Alexander, The Great
The first European to reach China	Marco Polo
The first person to fly aeroplane	Wright Brothers
The first person to sail round the world	Magellan
The first country to send man to the moon	U.S.A.
The first country to launch Artificial satellite in the space	Russia

The first country to host the modern Olympics	Greece
The first city on which the atom bomb was dropped	Hiroshima (Japan) (6th Aug. 1945)
The first person to land on the moon	Neil Armstrong followed by Edwin E. Aldrin
The first shuttle to go in space	Columbia
The first spacecraft to reach on Mars	Viking-1
The first woman Prime Minister of England	Margaret Thatcher
The first muslim woman Prime Minister of a country	Benazir Bhutto (Pakistan)
The first woman Prime Minister of a country	Mrs. S. Bhandarnaike (Sri Lanka)

The first woman to climb Mount Everest	Mrs. Junko Tabei (Japan)
The first woman cosmonaut of the world	Velentina Tereshkova (Russia)
The first woman President of the U.N. General Assembly	Vijaya Lakshmi Pandit
The first man to fly into space	Yuri Gagarin (Russia)
The first batsman to score three test century in three successive tests on debut	Mohd. Azharuddin
The first man to have climbed Mount Everest twice	Nawang Gombu
The first U.S. President to resign Presidency	Richard Nixon

FIRST IN INDIA	
Male	
The first President of Indian Republic	Dr. Rajendra Prasad
The first Prime Minister of free India	Pt. Jawahar Lal Nehru
The first Indian to win Nobel Prize	Rabindranath Tagore
The first President of Indian National Congress	W. C. Banerjee
The first Muslim President of Indian National Congress	Badruddin Tayyabji
The first Muslim President of India	Dr. Zakir Hussain
The first British Governor General of India	Lord William Bentinck
The first British Viceroy of India	Lord Canning The first Governor General of free India Lord Mountbatten
The first and the last Indian to be Governor General of free India	C. Rajgopalachari
The first man who Introduced printing press in India	James Hicky
The first Indian to join the I.C.S.	Satyendra Nath Tagore
India's first man in space	Rakesh Sharma
The first Prime Minister of India who resigned without completing the full term	Morarji Desai
The first Indian Commander-in-Chief of India	General Cariappa
The first Chief of the Army Staff	Gen. Maharaj Rajendra Singhji
The first Indian member of the Viceroy's executive council	S. P. Sinha
The first President of India who died while in office	Dr. Zakir Hussain

The first Prime Minister of India who did not face the Parliament	Charan Singh
The first Field Marshal of India	S. H. F. Manekshaw
The first Indian to get Nobel prize in Physics	C. V. Raman
The first Indian to receive Bharat Ratna award	Dr. Radhakrishnan
The first Indian to cross English channel	Mihir Sen
The first person to receive Gynanpith award	Sri Shankar Kurup
The first Speaker of the Lok Sabha	Ganesh Vasudeva Mavalankar
The first Vice-president of India	Dr. Radhakrishnan
The first Education Minister	Abul Kalam Azad
The first Home Minister of India	Sardar Vallabh Bhai Patel
The first Indian Air Chief Marshal	S. Mukherjee
The first Indian Naval Chief	Vice Admiral R. D. Katari
The first judge of international Court of Justice	Dr. Nagendra Singh
The first person to receive Paramveer Chakra	Major Somnath Sharma
The first person to reach Mount Everest without oxygen	Sherpa Anga Dorjee
The first Chief Election Commissioner	Sukumar Sen
The first person to receive Magsaysay Award	Acharya Vinoba Bhave
The first person of Indian origin to receive Nobel Prize in Medicine	Hargovind Khurana
The first Chinese traveller to visit India	Fahein
The first person to receive Stalin Prize	Saifuddin Kitchlu
The first person to resign from the central cabinet	Shyama Prasad Mukherjee
The first foreigner to receive Bharat Ratna	Khan Abdul Ghaffar Khan
The first person to receive Nobel Prize in Economics	Amartya Sen
The first Chief Justice of Supreme Court	Justice Hiralal J. Kania
Female	
The first lady to become "Miss World"	Rita Faria
The first woman judge in Supreme Court	Mrs. Meera Sahib Fatima Bibi
The first woman Ambassador	Miss C.B. Muthamma
The first woman Governor of a State in free India	Mrs. Sarojini Naidu
The first woman Prime Minister	Mrs. Indira Gandhi
The first woman to climb Mount Everest	Bachhendri Pal
The first woman to climb Mount Everest twice	Santosh Yadav
The first woman President of the Indian National Congress	Mrs. Annie Besant
The first woman chief justice of a High Court	Mrs. Leela Seth
The first woman pilot in Indian Air Force	Harita Kaur Dayal
The first woman President of the United Nations General Assembly	Mrs. Vijaya Laxmi Pandit
The first woman Chief Minister of an Indian State	Mrs. Sucheta Kripalani

The first woman chairman of Union Public Service Commission	Roze Millian Bethew
The first woman Director General of Police (DGP)	Kanchan Chaudhary Bhattacharya
The first woman Lieutenant General	Puneeta Arora
The first woman Air vice Marshal	P Bandopadhyaya
The first woman chairperson of Indian Airlines	Sushma Chawla
The first woman I.P.S. Officer	Mrs. Kiran Bedi
The first and the last Muslim woman ruler of Delhi	Razia Sultan
The first woman to receive Ashoka Chakra	Nirja Bhanot
The first woman to cross English Channel	Aarti Saha
The first woman to receive Nobel Prize	Mother Teresa
The first woman to receive Bharat Ratna	Mrs. Indira Gandhi
The first woman to receive Gyanpith Award	Ashapurna Devi

POPULAR NAMES OF PERSONALITIE S

Popular Name	Personality
Lady with the lamp	Florence Nightingale
Grand Old man of India	Dadabhai Naoroji
Iron Duke	Duke of Wellington
Guru Ji	M.S. Golwalkar
John Bull	England and the English people
CR	Chakravarti Rajagopalachari
King Maker	Earl of Warwick
JP	Jayaprakash Narayan
Little Corporal	Napoleon
Mahamana	Pt. Madan Mohan Malaviya
Gurudev	Rabindranath Tagore
Maid of Orleans	Joan of Arc
Desh Bandhu	C.R. Das
Deen Bandhu	C.F. Andrews
Yankee	Inhabitants of U.S.A
Lion of the Punjab (Sher-e-Punjab)	Lala Lajpat Rai
Bard of Avon	Shakespeare
Panditji	Jawaharlal Nehru
Man of Blood	Bismark
Andhra Kesri	T. Prakasam
Popular Name	**Personality**
Lokmanya	Bal Gangadhar Tilak
Bapu	Mahatma Gandhi
Apostle of Free Trade	Richard Cobden
Netaji	Subhash Chandra Bose
Desert Fox	Gen. Rommel
Nightingle of India	Sarojini Naidu
Lat, Bal. Pal	Lala Lajpat Rai, Bal Gangadhar Tilak, Bipin Chandra Pal
Father of English Poetry	Geoffery Chaucer
Feuhrer	Hitler
Iron man	Sardar Vallabh Bhai Patel
Wizard of the North	Sir Walter Scot
Samuel Clemens	Mark Twain
Sparrow	Major Gen.Rajender Singh
Shastriji	Lal Bahadur Shastri
Babuji	Jagjiwan Ram

GEOGRAPHICAL DISCOVERIES

Discovery	Discoverer	Discovery	Discoverer
America	Christopher Columbus	New Foundland	Gobot Sebastian
Sea route to India via Cape of Good Hope	Vasco-de-Gama	Hudson Bay	Henry Hudson
Solar system	Copernicus	Sailor of the world	Magellan
Planets	Kepler	Mount Everest	Edmund Hillary
South Pole	Amundsen	First person to set foot on the moon	Neil Armstrong
North Pole	Robert Peary	Tasmania island	Tasman
China	Marco Polo	Cape of the Good Hope	Baurtho Romeiodeis

CAPITALS AND CURRENCIES Of COUNTRIES

Country	Capital	Currency	Country	Capital	Currency
ASIA					
Afghanistan	Kabul	Afghani	Cambodia	Phnom Penh	Riel
Bahrain	Manama	Bahraini Dinar	Kazakhstan	Akmola	Tenge
Bangladesh	Dhaka	Taka	North Korea	Pyongyang	Won (KPW)
Bhutan	Thimpu	Ngultrum	Korea (South)	Seoul	Won (KRW)
China	Beijing	Yuan	Lebanon	Beirut	Lebnanese Pound
India	New Delhi	Indian Rupee	Malaysia	Kuala Lumpur	Malaysian Ringgit
Indonesia	djakarta	Rupiah	Maldives	Male	Rufiyaa
Iran	Tehran	Riyal	Mangolia	Ulan-Bator	Tugrik
Iraq	Baghdad	Iraqi Dinar	Myanmar	Yangoon	Kyat
Israel	Jerusalem	Shekel	Nepal	Kathmandu	Nepalese Rupee
Japan	Tokyo	Yen	Oman	Muscat	Omani Rial
Jordan	Amman	Jordan Dinar	Pakistan	Islamabad	Pakistani Rupee
Taiwan	Taipei	New Taiwan	Tajikistan	Dushambe	Tajik Rouble
Philippines	Manila	Piso	Thailand	Bangkok	Baht
Qatar	Doha	Qatari Riyal	Turkey	Ankara	Turkish Lira
Saudi Arabia	Riyadh	Riyal (SAR)	Turkemenistan	Ashkabad (TMM)	Manat
Singapore	Singapore	Singapore Dollar	United Arab Emirates	Abu Dhabi	Dirham
Sri Lanka	Sri Jaya wordenapura Kotle	Sri Lankan Rupee	Uzbekistan	Tashkent	Som (UKS)
			Vietnam	Hanoi	Dong
Syria	Damascus	Syrian Pound	Yemen	Sana	Riyal (YER)

Country	Capital	Currency	Country	Capital	Currency
EUROPE					
Andorra	Andorra la- vella	Euro	Lithuania	Vilnius	Litas
			Luxemburg	Luxemburg	Euro
Armenia	Yerevan	Dram	Macedonia	Skopje	Dinar
Austria	Vienna	Euro	Malta	Valletta	Euro
Azerbaijan	Baku	Manat	Moldova	Chisinau	Leu
Belarus	Minsk	Russian Rouble	Monaco	Monaco	Euro
Belgium	Brussels	Euro	Montenegro	Podogorica	Euro
Bosnia-Herjego vina	Sarajevo	Dinar	Netherlands	The Hague	Euro
Norway	Oslo	Norwegian Krone	Bulgaria	Sofia	Lev
Croatia	Zagreb	Kuna	Poland	Warsaw	Zloty
Portugal	Lisbon	Euro			
Cyprus	Nicosia	Euro	Romania	Bucharest	Lei
Czech Republic	Prague	Koruna	Russia	Moscow	Rouble
Denmark	Copenhagen	Danish Krone	San Marino	San Marino	Italian Lira
Estonia	Tallinn	Euro	Slovakia	Bratislava	Euro
Finland	Helsinki	Euro	Slovenia	Ljubljana	Euro
France	Paris	Euro	Spain	Madrid	Euro
Georgia	Tbilisi	Lari	Sweden	Stockholm	Krona(SEK)
Germany	Berlin	Euro	Switzerland	Berne	Swiss Franc
Greece	Athens	Euro	Ukraine	Kiev	Karbovanets
Hungary	Budapest	Forint	United Kingdom	London	Pound Sterling
Iceland	Reykavik	Krona	Vatican City	Vatican City	Italian Lira
Ireland	Dublin	Euro	Italy	Rome	Euro
AFRICA					
Botswana	Gaborone	Pula	The Gambia	Banjul	Dalasi
Burkina Faso	Ouagadougou	Franc (CFA)	Ghana	Accra	Cedi
Burundi	Bujumbura	Burundi Franc	Guinea	Conakry	Guinean Franc
Cameroon	Yaoundi	Franc (CFA)	Guinea Bissau	Bissau	Peso
Cape Verde	Praia	Cape Verde Escudo	Kenya	Nairobi	Kenya Shilling
Central African Republic	Bangui	Franc (CFA)	Lesotho	Maseru	Loti

Country	Capital	Currency	Country	Capital	Currency
Chad	N' Djamena	Franc (CFA)	Liberia	Monorovia	Liberian Dollar
Comoros	Moroni	Comorian Franc	Libya	Tripoli	Libyan Dinar
Madagascar	Antananrivo	Malagasy Franc			
Congo	Brazzaville	Franc (CFA)	Malawi	Lilongwe	Kwacha
Ivory Coast	Yamous-soukro	Franc (CFA)	Mali	Bamako	Franc (CFA)
Djibouti	Djibouti	Djibouti Franc	Mauritania	Nouakchott	Ouguiya
Egypt	Cairo	Egyptian Pound	Somalia	Mogadishu	Shilling
Mauritius	Port Louis	Mauritius Rupee	South Africa	Cape Town	Rand
Morocco	Rabat	Dirham	Sudan	Khartoum	Pound
Mozambique	Maputo	Metical	Swaziland	Mbabane	Lilangeni
Namibia	Windhock	Rand	Tanzania	Dar-es-Salaam	Shilling
Niger	Niamey	Franc	Togo	Lome	Franc
Nigeria	Lagos	Naira	Tunisia	Tunis	Dinar
Rwanda	Kigali	Franc	Uganda	Kampala	Shilling
Senegal	Dakar	Franc	Zambia	Lusaka	Kwatcha
Seychelles	Victoria	Rupee	Zimbabwe	Harare	Zimbabwe Dollar
Sierra Leone	Freetown	Leone			
NORTHAMERICA					
Antigua and Barbuda	St. Johns	Dollar	Guatemala	Guatemala City	Quetzal
			Haiti	Port-au-Prince	Gourde
Bahamas	Nassau	Dollar	Honduras	Tegucigalpa	Lempira
Barbados	Bridgetown	Dollar	Jamaica	Kingston	Dollar
Belize	Belmopan	Dollar	Mexico	Mexico City	Peso
Canada	Ottawa	Canadian Dollar	Nicaragua	Managua	Cordoba
Panama	Panama City	Balboa			
Costa Rica San	Jose	Colon	St. Kits and Nevis	Basseterre	Dollar
Cuba	Havana	Peso	Trinidad and Tobago	Port-of-Spain	Dollar
Dominica	Roseau	Sterling	El Salvador	San Salvador	Colon
United States of America	Washington (D.C.)	Dollar	Grenada	St. George	Dollar

Country	Capital	Currency	Country	Capital	Currency
SOUTH AMERICA					
Argentina	Buenos Aires	Austral (Pesu)	Paraguay	Asuncion	Guarani
Bolivia	La Paz	Boliviano	Peru	Lima	Nuevosol
Brazil	Brasilia	Cruzeiro	Surinam	Paramaribo	Guilder
Chile	Santiago	Peso	Uruguay	Montevideo	Peso
Ecuador	Quito	S-ore	Venezuela	Caracas	Boliver
Guyana	Georgetown	Dollar	French Guyana	Koenne	Franc
OCEANIA					
Australia	Canberra	Australian Dollar	Papua New Guinea	Port Moresby	Kina
Fiji	Suva	Fiji Dollar	Solomon Island	Honiara	Dollar
Nauru	Nauru	Dollar	Tonga	Nukualofa	Panga
NewZealand	Willington	New Zealand Dollar			

UNITED NATIONS ORGANISATION

- World's largest international organisation and a successor of League of Nations. (League of Nations was formed after the I World War, but it failed).
- The Charter of the UN was signed at San Francisco on June 26, 1945, at a meeting of the representatives of 50 states, representing 2/3rd of the world population.
- The Charter or Constitution was formed at Dumbarton Oaks (Washington DC) Conference by USSR, UK, US and China.
- Formally came into existence on Oct 24, 1945.
- First regular session was held in London in Jan,1946 and Trygve Le (Norway) was elected the first Secretary General.
- Headquarters located at First Avenue, UN Plaza, New York City, New York, US.
- The present membership of UN is 192. Switzerland was The 190th (in 2002), East Timor was the 191st (in 2002), while Montenegro became the 192nd member in 2006.
- US, UK, China, France and Russia are the permanent members of the Security Council.
- The present Secretary General of UN is Mr. Ban ki Moon of South Korea.

SOME IMPORTANT U.N. AGENCIES

Name of Agency	Estd.in	Headquarters	Purpose
International Labour Organisation (ILO)	1919	Geneva	To improve living conditions and standard of workers.
World Health Organisation (WHO)	1948	Geneva	Attainment of highest possible level of health by all people.

Name of Agency	Estd.in	Headquarters	Purpose
United Nations Educational, Scientific and Cultural Organisation (UNESCO)	1946	Paris	To promote collaboration among nations through education, science and culture.
International Atomic Energy Agency (IAEA)	1957	Vienna	To promote peaceful Energy uses of atomic energy.
United Nations International Children's Emergency Fund(UNICEF)	1946	New York	To promote children's welfare all over the world.
United Nations Conference on Trade and Development . (UNCTAD)	1964	Geneva	Promotes international trade to accelerate economic growth of developing countries.
International Civil Aviation Organisation (ICAO)	1947	Montreal	Promotes safety of international aviation.
International Monetary Fund (IMF)	1945	Washington D.C.	Promotes international monetary cooperation.
United Nations Environmental Programme (UNEP)	1972	Nairobi	Promotes international co-operation in human environment.
United Nations Industrial Development Organisation(UNIDO)	1967	Geneva	Sets international regulations for radio, telegraph, telephone and space radio communication.
International Bank for Reconstruction and Development (IBRD)	1945	Washington D.C.	Development of economies of members by facilitating investment of capitals by providing loans.
World Meteorological Organisation (WMO)	1950	Geneva	Promote international exchange of weather reports.
World Trade Organisation (WTO)	1995	Geneva	Setting rules for world trade to reduce tariffs.
United Nations Development Programme (UNDP)		New York	Help developing countries increase the wealth producing capabilities of their natural and human resources.

OTHER INTERNATIONAL ORGANISATIONS AND GROUPS

The CommonWealth

- It was originally known as The British Commonwealth of Nations'. It is an association of sovereign and independent states which formally made up the British empire.
- Headquarters : London.
- Members states : 53
- The British Monarch (Queen Elizabeth II) is the symbolic head of the commonwealth.
- Commonwealth heads of government meet (CHOGM) is held in every 2 years.

Asia Pacific Economic Cooperation (APEC)

- Established : Nov. 1989
- Objective : To promote trade and investment in the Pacific basin.
- Members : 21

Asian Development Bank (ADB)

- Established : Dec. 19, 1966
- Objective : To promote regional economic cooperation.
- Members : 67
- Headquarters: Manila, Philippines

Association of South-East Asian Nations (ASEAN)

- Established : Aug. 8, 1967
- Objective : Regional, economic, social and cultural cooperation among the non-communist countries of South-East Asia.
- Members : Brunei, Indonesia, Malaysia, Philippines, Singapore, Thailand, Vietnam, Laos, Myanmar, Cambodia.
- Headquarters : djakarta, Indonesia

Group of 7 or G-7

- Established : Sept. 22, 1985
- Objective : To promote co-operation among major non-communist economic powers.
- Members : France, Germany, Japan, UK, US, Canada and Italy.

Group of 15 (G-15)

- Established : 1989
- Objective : To promote economic co-operation among developing nations.
- Members :18

Group of 77(G-77)

- Established : Oct., 1967
- Objective: To promote economic co-operation among developing nations.
- Members : 132

International Criminal Police Organisation (INTERPOL)

- Established : 1923
- Objective : To promote international cooperation among criminal police authorities
- Members : 190
- Headquarters : Lyon, France

Internationl Olympic Committee (IOC)

- Established : June 23, 1894
- Objective: To promote the Olympic ideals and administer Olympic games.
- Members : 105 active members 32 honorary members
- Headquarters : Lausanne, Switzerland

International Organisation For Standardisation (ISO)

- Established : 23 Feb, 1947
- Objective : To promote the development of international standards.
- Members : 163
- Headquarters : Switzerland

International Red Cross And Red Crescent Movement

- Established : 24 June 1863
- Objective : To promote worldwide humanitarian aid.
- Headquarters : Geneva, Switzerland.

European Union

- Established : April 8, 1965. Effective on July 1. 1967.

- Objective : To create a united Europe in which member countries would have such strong economic and political bonds that war would cease to be a recurring fact.
- Members : 27 (The ten new countries which joined in 2004 are Cyprus, Czech Republic, Estonia, Hungary, Latvia, Lithuania. Malta, Poland, Slovakia and Slovania).
- Headquarters : Brussels (Belgium). The common European, currency. Euro, was launched on Jan. 1, 1999.

North Atlantic Teaty Organisation (NATO)

- Established : April 4, 1949
- Objective : Mutual defence and cooperation
- Members : 28
- Headquarters : Brussels, Belgium

Organisation of Petroleum Exporting Countries (OPEC)

- Established : Sept., 1959
- Objective : Attempts to set world prices by controlling oil production and also persues member interest in trade and development.
- Members : 12 (Algeria, Iran, Iraq, Kuwait, Libya, UAE, Nigeria, Qatar, Saudi Arabia, Ecuador and Venezuela).
- Headquarters : Vienna (Austria)

Sount Asian Association For Regional Cooperation (SAARC)

- Established : Dec. 8, 1985
- Objective : To promote economic, social and cultural cooperation
- Members : Bangladesh, Bhutan, India, Maldives, Nepal, Pakistan. Srilanka & Afghanistan.
- Headquarters : Kathmandu

World Meteorological Organisation (WMO)

- Established : Oct. 11, 1947, Effective from April 4, 1951.
- Objective : Specialised UN Agency concerned with meteorological cooperation.
- Members : 191
- Headquarters : Geneva, Switzerland

Shanghai Cooperation Organisation (SCO)

- Established : June 7, 2002.
- Objective : To develop mutual cooperation.
- Members : Russia, China, Kazakhistan, Uzbekistan, Kyrghiztan and Tajikistan.

Brics (Brazil, Russia, India, China, South Africa)

- Established : 2010 before inclusion of South Africa it is know as BRIC, which is established in 2009.
- Objective : To encouring commercial, political and cultural cooperation between BRICS nations.

WORLD : MISCELLANEOUS

- **NATIONAL EMBLEMS OF FAMOUS COUNTRIES**

Country	Emblem	Country	Emblem
Australia	Kangaroo	Italy	White Lily
Bangladesh	Water Lily	Japan	Chrysanthemum
Canada	White Lily	Norway	Lion
Denmark	Beach	Pakistan	Crescent
France	Lily	Spain	Eagle
Germany	Corn Flower	Sri Lanka	Sword & Lion
India	Lion Capital	Russia	Sickle & Hammer
Iran	Rose	United Kingdom	Rose
Ireland	Shamrock	U.S.A.	Golden Rod

• PARLIAMENTS NAME OF THE FAMOUS COUNTRIES

Country	Parliament	Country	Parliament
Afghanistan	Shora	Malaysia	Majlis
Australia	Parliament	Maldive	Majlis
Bangladesh	Jatia Parliament	Mangolia	Khural
Bhutan	Tasongadu	Nepal	Rasthtriya Panchayat
Canada	Parliament	Netherlands	States General
China	National People Congress	Norway	Storting
Denmark	Folketing	Pakistan	National Assembly
Egypt	People's Assembly	Poland	Scym
France	National Assembly	Spain	Crotes
Germany	Bundestag	Sweden	Riksdag
Great Britain	Parliament	South Africa	Parliament
India	Parliament (Sansad)	Switzerland	Federal Assembly
Iran	Majlis	Russia	Duma
Ireland	Dail Eireann	Taiwan	Yuan
Israel	Knesset	Turkey	Grand National Assembly
Japan	Diet	U.S.A.	Congress

• WONDERS OF THE WORLD

Ancient	Medieval
Hanging Gardens of Babylon	Colosseum of Rome
Temple of Diana at Ephesus (Rome)	Great Wall of China
Statue of Jupiter at Olympia	Porcelain Tower of Nanking
Mausoleum of Mausolus (Rular of Halicarnassus)	Stonehange of England
Pyramids of Egypt	Mosque at St. Sophia (Constantinople)
Light House at Alexandria	Catacombs of Alexandria
Colossus of Rhodes	Leaning Tower of Pisa
	Taj Mahal (India)

INDIAN DEFENCE

- The President of India is the supreme commander of the Indian Defence System.
- The whole administrative control of the Armed forces lies in the Ministry of Defence.
- Indian Defence System has been divided into three services-Army, Navy and Air Force.
- The **Indian Army** is organised into seven commands :

Commands	Headquarters
1. Western Command	Chandi Mandir
2. Eastern Command	Kolkata
3. Northern Command	Udhampur
4. Southern Command	Pune
5. Central Command	Lucknow
6. Army Training Command	Shimla
7. South Western Command	Jaipur

- **Indian air force is organised into seven commands :**

Commands	Headquarters
1. Western Command	New Delhi
2. Central Command	Allahabad
3. Eastern Command	Shillong
4. South Western Command	Jodhpur
5. Training Command	Bangaluru
6. Maintenance Command	Nagpur
7. Southern Command	Thiruvananthapuram

- **Indian navy is organised into three commands :**

Commands	Headquarters
Eastern Command	Vishakhapatnam
Southern Command	Kochi
Western Command	Mumbai

RANKS OF COMMISSIONED OFFICERS

Army	Air Forces	Navy
General	Air Chief Marshal	Admiral
Lt. General	Air Marshal	Vice Admiral
Major General	Air Vice Marshal	Rear Admiral
Brigadier	Air Commodore	Commodore
Colonel	Group Captain	Captain
Lt. Colonel	Wing Commander	Commander
Major	Squadron Leader	Lt. Commander
Captain	Flt. Lieutenant	Lieutenant
Lieutenant	Flying Officer	Sub-Lieutenant

■■

INDIAN HISTORY

ANCIENT INDIA

STONE AGE : THE EARLY MAN

1. PALEOLITHIC AGE

- Earth is over 4000 million years old. Evolution of its crust shows four stages.
- Fourth stage is called *Quaternary, which is divided into* (*i*) Pleistocene (most recent) lasted between 2,000,000 and 10,000 years before the present. (*ii*) *Holocene (present)* began about 10,000 years age.

2. MESOLITHIC AGE

- Upper Palaeolithic age came to an end with the end of Ice age around 9000 B.C. and the climate became warm and dry.
- In 9000 B.C. began an intermediate stage in stone age culture, which is called *Mesolithic age.*
- Mesolithic people lived on hunting, fishing and food gathering.
- Mesolithic culture continued to be important roughly from 9000 B.C. to 4000 B.C.

3. NEOLITHIC AGE

- The only neolithic settlement in the Indian subcontinent attributed to 7000 B.C. lies in Mehrgarh, which is situated in *Baluchistan,* a province of Pakistan.
- Neolithic phase in south India seems to have covered the period **from about** 2000 B.C. to about 1000 B.C.

4. CHALCOLITHIC AGE

- *Chalcolithic* means the stone-copper phase.
- Chalcolithic people mostly used stone and copper objects, but they also occasionally used low-grade bronze.
- The Jorwe Culture, 1400 B.C. to 700 B.C., covered modern Maharashtra except part of Vidarbha and the coastal region of Konkan.

Important Sites of Harappan Civilisation

Site	Location	River bank
Harappa	Montegomari, Punjab (Pakistan)	Ravi
Mohenjodaro	Larkana, Sindh (Pakistan)	Indus
Kotdiji	Sindh (Pakistan)	Indus
Lothal	Ahmedabad	Sabarmati & Bhogva
Alamgirpur	Meerut(UP)	Hindon
Banawali	Hissar (Haryana)	Saraswati
Sutkagendor	Baluchistan (Pakistan)	Dashto
Chanhudaro	Sindh (Pakistan)	Indus
Rangpur	Ahmedabad (India)'	Meedar
Ropar	Punjab (India)	—
Kalibangan	Ganganagar (Rajasthan)	Ghaggar

Note: *Most number of sites are found in Gujarat.*

GENERAL FACTS ABOUT SOME SITES

1. **Harappa**
    - Six granaries and sixteen *agnikundas* (firepits) have been found here.
    - People of Harappa knew the process of making tarcoal.
    - Main gate for the entry in the houses of Harappa was in the north direction.
    - Terracotta figurine of Mother Goddess have been found here.
2. **Mohenjodaro**
    - Mohenjodaro was discovered in 1922 under the supervision of R.D. Bannerji.
    - Seven layers of Mohenjodaro city directs that the city was destroyed and rebuilt seven times.
    - The meaning of Mohenjodaro in Sindhi language is **mound of the dead**.
    - The **Great Bath, a granary, big halls**, a bronze statue of a dancing girl, idol of a yogi and have been found here.
    - The evidences of a assembly hall and proper planned houses with a kitchen and courtyard have been found at Mohenjodaro.
3. **Lothal**
    - Lothal was discovered by S.R. Rao Gulf of Cambay in Gujarat, in 1957.
    - A dockyard have been found at Lothal.
    - Copper tools, red & black clay pots, brick built tank like structure, a bead making factory and a seal from Iran have been found at Lothal.
    - Linear scale of bronze have been found here.
3. **Kalibangan**
    - Kalibangan was discovered in 1953. It is located in upper Rajasthan.
    - It saw two cultural phases viz. pre-Harappan and Harappan.
    - A ploughed field have been found here.
    - It did not have a drainage system.
    - A number of firepits *agnikundas* (firepits) have been found here.

VEDIC PERIOD

Rig/Early Vedic Period (500-1000 BC)

Geographical area

- The Aryans were semi-nomadic pastoral people and originally believed to live somewhere in the **Steppes** stretching from Southern Russia to Central Asia.
- As per the Rigved the whole region in which the Aryans were first settled in India, called the **Land of 7 Rivers** or **Sapta Sindhawa.**

Political Organization

- **The Dasrajan War** Battle of ten kings against Sudas (Bharata king of Tritsus) on the bank of river Parushni. Sudas emerged victorious.
- It was mainly tribal system of government in which the military element was strong.
- Tribe was called as **Jan** and its chief as **Rajan.**
- Traces of election of the King by the assembly, called **Samiti,** Rogal officials were senani (army chief) and Villages were headed by **Gramini.**
- In day-to-day administration, King was assisted by **Purohita** (most important), (Vishwamitra, Vasishtha) a **Senani** and **Vrata, Gana, Grama** and **Sardha** (tribal groups performing various military functions).

Religion

- Worshipped Indra (also called Purandara-breaker of foots) was the most important divinity also played the role of a warlord and considered to be the rain god.
- **Soma** was considered to be the god of plants.
- People worshipped mainly for **Praja** (children), **Pashu** (cattle), food, health and wealth. No temple or idol worship.
- Agni, next to indra, acted as a kind of intermedeate between god and the people.

Economy

No regular revenue system, kingdom maintained by voluntary tribute called bali and booty won in battles.

- Aryans' main occupation-cattle rearing, people agriculture being secondary.

- Cow was standard unit of exchange. Gold coins-Nishka, Krishnal and Satmana. Cow was also called aghnya (not to be killed)
- The staple crop was **yava** (barley). Wheat was secondary crop.

Rigvedic Terms

Rigvedic Term	Meaning
• Kalapas	over large tract of land
• Gramini	Lead of the family
• Gavisthi	Fighting hordes, Search for cows/war for cows
• Dasyus	Original inhabitant of India
• Ayas	Copper/bronze
• Vajrapati	Officer enjoying authority

Rigvedic Rivers

Rivar	Name in Rigveda
• Sutlej	Sutudri
• Gomati	Gomal
• Saraswati	Sarasvati
• Ghaggar	Prishadavati
• Indus	Sindhu
• Jhelum	Vitasta
• Chenab	Asikni
• Ravi	Parushini
• Beas	Vipasa

Later Vedic Period (1000-500 BC)

- In this period, Aryans expanded from Punjab over the whole of Western Uttar Pardesh covered by the Ganga-Yamuna Doab.

Political Organization

- King *(Samrat)* became more powerful and tribal authority tended to become territorial.
- King position strengthened by rituals like **Ashwamedha** and **Vajapeya Yajnas.**

Society

- Society clearly divided into four varnas—Brahmana, Kshatriya, Vaishya and Shudra. Position of women deteriorated.
- The institution of Gotra (descent from common ancestors) appeared for the first time.

Economy

- Beginning of town and settled life.
- Agriculture was the main livelihood. Rice (Vrihi) and wheat (Godhana) was the chief crops of the later vadic organs through they continued to produce Barley (yava)
- Occupations like ironsmith, coppersmith, jewel workers and weaving (reserved for women). Leather work, Pottery and carpenter's work made great progress.

Religion

- **Prajapati** became the supreme God followed by **Rudra** (animal God), **Vishnu** (preserver and protector of people).
- **Pushan** who looked after cattles was 'God of Shudras'.
- Sacrifices rather than prayers became more important.

Vedic Literature

The Vedas

- **Rigveda** oldest Indo-European language text is a collection of hymns. Contains 1028 hymns and 10 mandalas.
- 10th Mandala contains four varnas or **Purushukta** whereas 3rd Mandala contains **Gayatri mantra** dedicated to Sun God. Savitri, IX dedicated to Soma god.
- **Samaveda** Collection of melodies : contains **Dhrupad raga.** Contains 1810 hymns.
- **Yajurveda** Contains hymns and rituals/ sacrifices.
- **Atharvaveda** Charms and spells to ward-off evils and diseases, Ayurveda has its organ from Atharvaved.

The Aranyakas

The word *Aranya* means the forest work called Aranyakas because they were written mainly for the hermits and students living in jungle.

The Upanishads

(to sit down near someone)

Philosophical texts emphasising value of **right belief** and **knowledge;** criticized rituals/ sacrifices; and are 108 in number. Vribadaranyaka is the oldest upanishads.

Smritis

Explains rules and regulations in Vedic life. These are **Manusmriti** (the first law book), **Naradsmriti, Yagyavalkyasmriti and Parasharsmriti.**

Vedangas

Limbs of Vedas are six in number. These are

Vedanga	Meaning	Vedanga	Meaning
Shiksha	pronunciation	Nirukta	etymology
Kalpa	rituals	Chandha	metre
Vyakarna	grammar	Jyotisha	astronomy

Darshans

There are six schools of Indian philosophy called **Shad-Darshana.** These are

Darshan	Given by
• Nyaya Darshana	Gautam
• Vaisheshika Darshana	Kanada Rishi
• Sankhya Darshana	Kapila
• Yoga Darshana	Kapila
• Purva Mimansa	Jaimini
• Uttar Mimansa	Badrayna or Vyasa
• Lokayata	Charvaka

Upavedas

There are four Upavedas

Upaveda	Deals with	Upaveda of
Dhanurveda	art of warfare	Yajurveda
Gandharvaveda	art & music	Samaveda
Shilpaveda	architecture	Atharvaveda
Ayurveda	medicine	Rigveda

Mahajanapadas

Mahajanapada	Capital
• Kashi	Varanasi
• Anga	Champanagri
• Vajji	Vaishali
• Chedi	Shuktimati
• Kuru	Hastinapur
• Matoya	Viratnagar
• Assaka	Budanya
• Gandhara	Taxila
• Kosala	Shravasti
• Magadh	Rajagriha
• Malla	Kushinagar
• Vatsa	Kaushambi
• Panchala	Ahichhatra
• Surasena	Mathura
• Avanti	Ujjain
• Kamshaja	Rajpur

Epics

- **Mahabharata by Vyasa.** Also called Jaya Samhita and Satasahasri Samhita has 100000 verses and older than **Ramayana,** written by **Valmiki** which has 29000 verses.

JAINISM

- Founded by Rishabhadeva/Aadinath.
- There were 24 *Tirthankaras* (Prophets or Gurus), all Kshatriyas. First was Rishabhnath (Emblem: Bull). The 23rd Tirthankar Parshwanath (Emblem: Snake) was the son of King Ashvasena of Banaras.
- The 24th and the last Tirthankar was Vardhman Mahavira (Emblem: Lion). He was born in Kundagram (Distt Muzafflarpur, Bihar) in 599 BC.
- He was related to Bimbisara.
- He married to Yashoda and they had a daughter named Priyadarsena, whose husband Jamali became his first disciple.
- After the death of his parents, he became an ascetic at the age of 30.
- In the 13th year of his asceticism (on the 10th of Vaishakha), outside the town of Jimbhikgrama, he attained supreme knowledge *(Kaivalya).*
- He was called *Jaina* or *Jitendriya* and Mahavira, and his followers were named Jains also called Arihant, i.e., worthy.

- At the age of 72, Know as in 527 BC, the attained death at Pava, near Patna.
- Mahavira preached almost the same message as Parshvanath and added one more, *Brahmcharya* (celibacy) to it.
- **Five doctrines of Jainism**
  (*i*) Do not speak lie (Satya)
  (*ii*) Observe continence (Brahmacharya)
  (*iii*) Do not commit violence (Ahimsa)
  (*iv*) Do not steal (Asteya)
  (*v*) Do not acquire property (Aparigraha)
- **Triratnas of Jainism** Kaivalya can be attained through right faith and right conduct, **right knowledge**.
- Jainism recognized existence of God but lower than **Jina**.
- Jain monastic establishment were called **basadis.**
- Jainism was patronized by Kharavela the king of Kalinga; Chandragupta Maurya *(became disciple of Bhadrabahu and spread Jainism in South).*

Councils
- **First Council** (300 BC) of Patliputra Under Sthulbhadra (Patliputra) Jain canons compiled.
- **Second Council** at Vallabhi (AD 5th century) Under Kshamasramana *(Vallabhi)* 12 Angas and 12 Upangas compiled in **Ardh Magadhi language.**

- Jainism was divided into two sects after Vallabhi Council, namely **Svetambaras** {wearing white dresses) under Sthulbhadra and **Digambaras** *(naked)* under Bhadraba.
- Jain texts were written in **Prakrit** language. Ex 14 Purvas; 12 Angas.

BUDDHISM

THE BUDDHA

- Childhood name was Siddharth and also known as Sakyamuni Tathagata and Gautam Buddha.
- He was born in 563 BC on *the Vaishakha Poornima* Day at Lumbini (near Kapilavastu) in Nepal.
- His mother (Mahamaya, of Kosala dynasty) died after 7 days of his birth. Brought up by stepmother Gautami.
- Married at 16 to Yoshodhara. Enjoyed the married life till the age of 29 and had a son named Rahula.
- After seeing an old man, a sick man, a corpse and an ascetic, he decided to become a wanderer.
- In search of truth (also called *'Mahabhinish-kramana'* or The Great Renunciation) wandered for 6 years.
- At 35 attained 'Enlightenment' at Gaya in Magadha (Bihar) under the Pipal tree.
- Delivered the first sermon at Sarnath where his five disciples had settled. His first sermon is called *'Dharmachakra-pravartan'* or Turning of the Wheel of Law'.
- In 483 BC at the age of 80 in the Malla republic, attained *Mahaparinirvana* at Kushinagar (identical with village Kasia in Deoria district of UP).

The Dhamma

Buddhism The Four Great Truths

- The world is full of sorrow and misery.
- The cause of all pain and misery is desire.
- Pain and misery can be ended by killing or controlling desire.
- Desire can be controlled by following the Eight Fold Path.

The Eight Fold Path

• Right Understanding	Right Efforts
• Right Thought	Right Speech
• Right Action	Right Mindfullness
• Right Livelihood	Right Concentration

Belief in Nirvana

- When desire ceases, rebirth ceases and nirvana is attained *i.e.,* freedom from the cycle of birth, death and rebirth is gained by 8 fold path.

Phases of Buddha's Life	**Known as**
• Left home at the age of 29	Mahabhinishkraman a
• Under Peepal tree at Bodh Gaya at the age of 35	attained knowledge / enlightment / Nirvana
• First Sermon	Dharmachakra-parivartana
• Death	Mahaparinirvana

Belief in Ahimsa

- One should not cause injury to any living being, animal or man.

Law of Karma

- Man reaps the fruits of his past deeds.

Buddhist Literature

- In **Pali language** commonly referred to as **Tripitakas,** i.e., 'three fold basket'.

Vinaya Pitaka

- Rules of discipline in Buddhist monasteries.

Sutta Pitaka

- Largest, contains collection of Buddha's sermons.

Abhidhamma Pitaka

- Explanation of the philosophical principles of the Buddhist religion.

> **Mahavamsha** and **Dipavamsa** are the other Buddhist texts of Sri Lanka.

Dynasties of Ancient India

Haryanka Dynasty

- **Bimbisara** was the founder, who expanded the Magadha kingdom by annexing Anga and entering into matrimonial alliances with Kosala and Vaishali. He was contemporary of Buddha. Capital-Rajgir (Girivraja).
- **Ajatshatru,** son of Bembisar came to power by killing his father. Annexed Vaishali, Kosala and Lichchhavi kingdom.
- **Udayin** son of Ajatshatru founded the new capital, Patliputra.

Shishunaga Dynasty

- Founded by Shishunaga; succeeded by Kalashoka or Kakavarin who convened 2nd Buddhist council. In Vashali (383 BC). Their greatest achievement was destruction of the Prodotya dynasty of Avanti.

Nanda Dynastry

- Considered **non-Kshatriyan** dynasty, founded by **Mahapadma Nanda.** Alexander attacked during **Dhana Nanda** reign.
- **Alexander,** the king of Macedonia, invaded India in 326 BC and fought the Battle of Hydapses (Jhelum) with **Porus** (Purushottam) of **Paurava dynasty.**

Mauryan Dynasty

Chandragupta Maurya The first ruler who overthrew Dhananand of Nanda dynasty with the help of Chanakya.

- He has been called **Sandrocottus** by Greek scholars.
- Chandragupta defeated **Seleucus Nikator,** the general of Alexander (305 BC), who later sent **Megasthenese** the author of **'Indica'**–to Chandra-gupta's court as a ambassador.
- **Mudrarakshasa** was written by Vishakhadatta, describes about machinations of Chanakya against Chandragupta's enemy.
- Chandragupta maintained six wings of armed forces.
- He adopted jainism and went to **Sravanabelagola** with **Bhadrabahu.**
- Bindusara was called Amitraghat (*i.e.*, slayer of foes) by Greek writers; Greek ambassador, **Deimachos** visited his court; said to conquer the **'land between the two seas'**—The Arabian Sea and Bay of Bengal.

Ashoka

- Ashoka was appointed the Viceroy of Taxila and Ujjain by his father Bindusara.
- The name **Ashoka** occurs only in copies of Minor Rock Edict I.
- Languages (scripts) used on inscriptions—Brahmi (sub-continent, deciphered by **James Princep** in AD 1837), Aramic and Kharosti (North-Western India), and Greek (Afghanistan).
- Ashoka was the first king, who maintained direct contact with people through inscriptions.
- **Kalinga War** (261 BC) mentioned in 13th Major Rock Edict—converted Ashoka to Buddhism under **Upagupta.**

- **Sanchi Stupa** was built by Ashoka.
- The last Mauryan king **Brihadratha,** was killed by Pushyamitra Sunga in 185 BC, who established Sunga dynasty.
- The **punch-marked coins** carrying the symbol of the peacock, and the hill and crescent famed the imperial currency of Mauryas.
- The Mauryas artisans started the practice of hewing out caves of monks to live in **Barabar Caves** near Gaya is earliest example of such cave.
- **Ringwells** for domestic use of water appeared first under the Mauryas.

The Shakas

- The most famous ruler was **Rudradaman I** (AD 130-150), who repaired Sudarshana lake in **Kathiawar** region, issued first ever inscription in Chaste Sanskrit (Junagarh inscription). He defeated Satvahanas twice.
- **Vikramaditya,** the king of Ujjain, was the only one who defeated the Shakas. To commemorate the victory, he started **Vikram Samvat** in 57 BC.
- **The Parthians** The most famous king was Gondophernes (AD 19-45), in whose reign St Thomas visited India to Propagate Christianity.

The Kushans

- Also called **Yeuchi or Tocharians** were nomadic people from the Steppes.
- **Kanishka** was the greatest of the Kushans, also know as 'Second Ashok' who started the **Saka Era** in AD 78. Which is used by the Government of India.
- Kushans were the first rulers to issue **gold coins** on wide scale.
- In the royal court of Kanishka, a host of scholars found patronage, like Parsva, Vasumitra, Asvaghosha, Nagarjuna, Charak (Physician) and Mathara were some of them.

The Sunga Dynasty (185 BC - 73 BC)

- Sunga Dynasty was established by Pushyamitra Sunga. Who was a Brohmin Commander in chief of lost merurya Rular Brihadrath in 185 BC.
- **Patanjali,** wrote 'Mahabhasya', at this time.
- In arts, the Bharhut stupa is the most famous monument of the Sunga period.

The Kanva Dynasty (73 BC - 28 BC)

- In 73 BC, Devabhuti, the last ruler of the Sunga dynasty, was murdered by his minister Vasudeva, who usurped the throne and founded the Kanva dynasty.

The Satavahanas (or Andhras)

- Simuka (60 BC-37 BC) was the founder of the Satavahana dynasty, who replaced Kanva dynesty.
- Satavahanas were finally succeeded by the **Ikshvakus** in AD 3rd century.
- Under the Satavahanas, many chaityas (worship halls) and viharas (monastries) were cut out from rocks mainly in North-West Deccan or Maharashtra the famous examples were Nasik, Kanheri and Karle.
- The official language of the Satavahanas was **Prakrit.**
- The Satavahanas issued **coins** of lead (mainly), copper, bronze and potin.
- Gautamiputra Satakarni was the greatest rural (23rd Satruhan Rural).

The Pandyas

The Pandyas were first mentioned by Megasthanese, famous for pearls. Their capital was Madurai.

- Trade with Roman empire, sent embassies to emperor Augustus.

The Cholas

- The Chola kingdom called as Cholamandalam was situated to the North-East of Pandya Kingdom between Pennar and Vellar rivers. Capital was Kaveripattanam/puhar.

Sangam Age

- Sangam was a college or assembly of Tamil poets held under **Royal Patronage.**

  Three Sangams were held

  (*i*) at Madurai, chaired by Nakkirar.

  (*ii*) at Madurai chaired by Agastya.

  (*iii*) at Kapatpuram, chaired by Tolkappiyar.
- Sangam Age corresponds to the post-Maurya and pre-Gupta period.
- **Kural** by Tiruvalluvar is called the 'fifth Veda' or **The Bible of Tamil Land.**

Gupta Period

Chandragupta I (AD 319-334)

Married Lichchhavi princess who strengthened his position and enhanced Gupta's prestige.

- He was the first Gupta ruler to acquire the title of **Maharajadhiraja.**
- Chandragupta I was able to establish his authority ever Magadha, Prayaga and Saketa.

Samudragupta (AD 335-380)

- He is called the **Napoleon of India** (by VA Smith) on account of his violence and conquest.
- **Meghavarman** the ruler of Sri Lanka, sent a missionary to his court for permission to built a monestery for buddist pilgrims at Bodh goya.
- He assumed the titles of Kaviraj and Vikrama.

Chandragupta II (AD 380-414)

- **Mehrauli** iron pillar **inscription** near **Qutub Minar** is related to him.
- His court was adorned by **Navratnas,** the chief being **Kalidasa** and **Amarsimha, Fa-hien,** Chinese Pilgrim (AD 399-414) visited during his reign.
- Chandragupta II aslo succeeded in killing Rangupta, and not only seized his kingdom but also married to his widow Dhruvdevi.
- He was 'the first Gupta ruler to issued the silver coins' and adopted the titles Sakari and Vikramaditya in the memory of victory over Sakas.
- The Gupta age is called **golden age** of Indian history issued largest number of gold coins.

Kumargupta I (AD 415-455)

- Chandragupta II was succeeded by his son Kumargupta I.
- Kumargupta was the worshipper of God Kartikeya.
- He founded the **'Nalanda Mahavihara'** which developed into a great centre of learning.

Skandagupta (AD 455-467)

- Skandagupta, the last great ruler of the Gupta dynasty. During his reign the Gupta empire was invaded by the Huns.
- Success in repelling the Huns seems to have been celebrated by the assumption of the title 'Vikramaditya' (Bhitari Pillar Inscription.)
- The decline of empire began soon after the death.

Pushyabhuti Dynasty (AD 606-647)

- Founded by Pushyabhiti at Thaneswar
- The greatest king was **Harshavardhana,** son of Prabhakar Vardhana of **Thaneshwar.**
- Harshavardhana shifted the capital to **Kannauj.**
- Defeated by **Pulakesin II,** the great Chalukyan king of Vatapi in AD 620.
- **Hieun Tsang** visited during his reign.
- He established a large monastery at Nalanda. **Banabhata** adorned his court wrote **Harshacharita** and **Kadambari.** Harsha himself wrote three plays in Sanskrit— **Priyadarshika, Ratnawali** and **Nagananda.**

Rashtrakutas

- Founded by **Dantidurg;** Krishna I built Kailasha temple at **Ellora.**
- Amoghavarsha, who is compared to Vikramaditya, wrote the first Kannada poetry **Kaviraj Marg.**

- Rashtrakutas credited for building cave shrine **Elephanta** dedicated to Shiva.

Gangas

- Ruled Orissa; **Narsimhadeva** constructed **Sun Temple at Konark.**
- Anantvarman built the **Jagannath Temple at Puri** and Kesaris who used to rule before Gangas built the **Lingaraja Temple at Bhubaneshwar.**

Pallavas (575 - 897 AD)

- **Founder Simhavishnu;** capital-Kanchi; greatest king **Narsim-havarman** who founded the town of Mamallapurams (Mahabalipuram) and built rock-cut raths or even agodas.

The Cholas (850 - 1279 AD)

- Founder Vijayalaya, Capital Tanjore.
- **Aditya I** Chola wiped out Pallavas and weakened Pandayas.
- **Purantaka I** captured Madurai but defeated *by* Rashtrakuta *ruler* Krishna III at the Battle of Takkolam.
- **Rajaraja I** (AD 985-1014) led a naval expedition against Shailendra empire (Malaya Peninsula) and conquered Northern **Sri Lanka;** constructed Rajarajeshwari (or Brihadeshvara) Shiva temple at **Tanjore.**
- **Rajendra I** (AD 1014-1044) annexed whole Sri Lanka; took the title of Gangaikonda and founded **Gangaikonda Cholapuram.**
- **Dancing Figure of Shiva** (Nataraja) belong to Chola period.

DYNASTIES OF MEDIEVAL INDIA

Mahmud of Ghazni.

- Mahmud came to the thron of Ghazni in 997 AD.
- He led 17 expeditions between 1001 and 1027. He plundered Thaneshwar, Mathura, Kannauj and Somnath. Temple (dedicated to Shiva) in 1025 was famous, situated on the sea coast of Kathiarwar.
- He was not interested in expanding his empire to India but his objective was to plunder the riches of temples and palaces.

Mohammed Ghori.

- Prithviraj Chauhan, the king of Delhi at that time, defeated him in the **I Battle of Tarain** (1191), but Mohammad Ghori defeated Him in the **II Battle of Tarain** in 1192.
- He may be considered the "founder of muslim rule" in India, in 1206, murdered taken Qutab-ud-Din Aibak the charge.

THE ILBARI DYNASTY OR SLAVE DYNASTY (AD 1206 - 1290)

Qutab-Ud-Din Albak (1206 - 1210)

- Initial Lahore and later Delhi was his capital. Laid the foundation of Qutab Minar after the name of famous Sufi saint, Knwaja Qutbuddin Bakhtiyar Kaki.
- Built the first mosque in India-*Quwwat-ul-lstam* (Delhi) and *Adhai Din Ka Jhonpara* (at Ajmer).
- Died of a horse fall at Lahore, while playing *Chaugan* (polo) in 1210.

Iltutmish (1210 - 1236)

- He formed *Turkan-i-Chahalgani* or *Chalisa* (a group of 40 powerful Turkish nobles to suppress nobles).
- He introduced the silver *tanka* and the copper *jital* – 2 basic coins of the Sultanate.
- Divided his empire into *IQTAS,* an assignment of land in lieu of salary, which he distributed to his officers.

Raziya (1236-1240)

- She disregarded purdah, began to adorn male attire.
- She promoted Jalaluddin Yakut, an Abyssinian, to the important office superintendent of the stables. It provoked the Turkish officers.
- She had to marry Altunia (the Governor of Bhatinda).
- **Bahram Shah, a son of Iltutmish**, Killed her along with her husband.
- She was the first and the last Muslim woman ruler of medieval India.

Balban (1266-1286)

- He ordered the separation of military department from the finance department *(diwan-i-wizarat)*, and the former was placed under a ministry for military affairs *(diwan-i-ariz)*.

- He declared the Sultan as the representative of god on earth. The deputy of God *(niyabat-i-khudai)* and the shadow of God *(zil-i-ilahi)*.
- Introduced *Sijdah* and *Paibos* practice, in which the people were required to kneel and touch the ground with their head to greet the Sultan.

THE KHALJI DYNASTY

Jalaluddin Flruz Khalji (1290-1296)

- He was the first ruler to put forward the view that India can not be a totally Islamic state.

Alauddin Khalji (1296-1316)

- Built *Hauz Khas, Mahal Hazaar Satoon* and *Jamait Khana Mosque.*
- First Sultan to had permanent army — paid soldiers in cash, imported horses, detailed description of each soldier *(Chehra)* and each horse *(Dagh)* was kept (first time). His Land Revenue System is very famous.
- First Turkish Sultan of Delhi who separated religion from politics. He proclaimed - *"Kingship knows no kinship".*
- Though Alauddin was illiterate, he was a patron of learning and art. There were many great poets in his court. **Amir Khusrau** and **Mir Hasan Dehlvi** were two famous poet of his court..

TUGHLAQ DYNASTY (AD 1320 - 1413)

Ghiyasuddin Tughlaq (1320-1325)

- Built the fortified city of *Tughlqabad* and made it his capital.
- Was the first subtan to start irregation work.

Muhammad Bin Tughlaq (1325-1351)

- He Regarded as the most controversial figure in Indian history, **because of his five ambitious projects:**
  - **Increase in the land revenue In the Doab (1326) :** *The measure proved to be ill-timed, as Doab was passing through famine which was followed by plague,*
  - **Transfer of capital to Devagiri (Daulatabad) (1327) :** But *it was not possible to control North India from there. So he decided to retransfer the capital to Delhi.*
  - **Introduction of token currency (1329) :** *Introduction of bronze* **tankas** *in place of silver* ***tankas*** *with equal value. But this experiment failed, due to counterfeit coins. So he withdrew the scheme and all token coins were exchanged for silver coins.*
  - **Planning of expedition for the conquest of Khurasan and Iraq (1329) :** *But the scheme* was *abandoned as conditions in Iraq improved (paid the extra army for one full year).*
  - **The plan for the conquest of Qarachii (Kumaon hills) (1330) :** *It also met with a disastrous end.*
- The famous traveler, Ibn Batuta came is Delhi during 1334.

Firoz Shah Tughlaq (1351 - 1388)

- Built his capital *Firozabad* & to beautify it, brought 2 Ashoka Pillars, one from Topara in Ambala & the other from Meerut.
- Built new towns - Hissar, Firozpur, Fatehabad, Firoz Shah Kotla & Jaunpur.
- *'Fatuhat Firozshahi'* written by him.

THE SAYYID DYNASTY

- Khizr Khan founded this short-lived dynasty and claimed to have descended from Ihe prophet of Islam.
- Khizr Khan's 3 successors - Mubarak Shah (1421-33), Muhammad Shah (1434-43) S Alauddin Alam Shah (1443-51) were incapable leaders.

THE LODHI DYNASTY

Bahlul Lodhi (1451-1489)

- They were Afghans by race (considered the first Afghan dynasty of India).
- Revived Sultanate to quite an extent.

Sikandar Lodhi (1489 - 1517)

- Introduced the *Gaz-e-Sikandari* (Sikandar's yard) of 32 digits for measuring cultivated fields.
- In 1504, he founded the city of Agra and made it his capital.

Ibrahim Lodhi (1517-1526)

- Was defeated and killed by Babur in the I Battle of Panipat in 1526.

THE MUGHAL EMPIRE

Babur (1526 -1530)

- Founder of Mughal Dynasty.
- Defeated Ibrahim Lodi in the **First Battle of Panipat** in 1526 and introduced gunpowder in India.
- In 1527 defeated Sangram Singh (Rana Sanga) of Mewar in the **Battle of Khanua**.
- In 1528 defeated another Rajput ruler, Medini Rai (of Chanderi) in the **Battle of Chanderi**.
- In 1529 defeated the Afghan chiefs under Mahmud Lodi (brother of Ibrahim Lodi) in the **Battle of Ghagra**.
- Died in 1530. Buried at Aram Bagh in Agra; later his body was taken to Aram Bagh, Kabul.
- His memoir, the *Tazuk-i-Baburi* in Turki language is a classic of world literature.

Humayun (1530 - 1556)

- He did a blunder by dividing his empire among his three brothers-Kamran, Hindal and Askari.
- He was attacked by Sher Shah at *Chausa **(Battle of Chausa)*** in 1539, but escaped.
- But in the **Battle of Kannauj (or Bilgrama)** in 1540, he was defeated by Sher Shah and had to flee to Iran.
- Passed nearly 15 years (1540-1555) in exile.
- **Bairam Khan**, his most faithful officer, helped him in Chance to return in 1555.
- Died in 1556, due to a fall from his library building stairs *(Sher Mandal,* Delhi).
- Gulbadan Begum, his sister, wrote *Humayun-nama.*

Akbar (1556 - 1605)

- He was crowned when he was just 14 years old.
- Bairam Khan represented him in the **Second Battle of Panipat** in 1556 against Hemu Vikramaditya. In which Hemu was defeated.
- Akbar ruled under Bairam Khan's regency between 1556-1560.
- Married Raja Bharmal's daughter, Jodha Bai in 1562 which paved the way for friendship between Rajputs and Mughals (except Mewar).
- Won Gujarat in 1572. It was in order to commemorate his victory of Gujarat that Akbar got the *Buland Darwaza* constructed at *Falehpur Sikri.*
- Fought **Battle of Haldighati** with Maharana Pratap in which Maharana was defeated.
- Formulated an order called *Din-i-Ilahi or Tauhid-i-llahi* in 1582. Birbal, Abul Fazal and Faizi joined the order.
- His Land Revenue System was known as *Todar Mal Bandobast or* **Zabti System.**

Jahangir (1605 - 1627)

- He executed, the fifth Sikh guru, Guru Arjun Dev, who had helped the revolting prince Khusrau.
- His greatest failure was the loss of Kandahar to Persia in 1622.
- He married Mehr-un-Nisa, the widow of Sher Afghani in 1611. The title of *NurJahan* was conferred on her.
- **Captain Hawkins** (1608-11) and **Sir Thomas Roe** (1615-1619) visited his court.
- During his reign tobacco growing started. It was brought by the Portuguese.
- During his reign painting reached its zenith.

Shahjahan (1628 - 1658)

- His reign is considered the **'Golden Age'** of the Mughal Empire.

- Built Red Fort at Delhi and Jama Masjid, Tajmahal, Moti Masjid at Agra etc.
- During the last days of his reign there was a brutal war of succession among his four sons (Dara, Shuja, Aurangzeb and Murad). Shahjahan liked Dara, but Aurangzeb came out victorious. Thus, Shahzahan had to spend last 8 years of his life in prison in Agra fort where he died in capivity in 1666 and barried at Taj (Agra).

Aurangzeb (1658 - 1707)

- Various rebellions took place - Satnami peasantry in Punjab and Bundelas in Bundelkhand and jat peasantry at Mathura.
- He caused serious rift in the Mughal-Rajput alliance by his policy of annexation of Marwar in 1639 after the death of Raja Jaswant Singh.
- In 1675, he ordered the arrest and execution of ninth Sikh guru, Guru Tegh Bahadur, when Guru Teg Bahadur refused to embrace Islam.
- The Mughal conquests reached the territorial climax during his reign. The Mughal empire stretched from Kashmir in the north to Jinji in the south, from the Hindukush in the west to Chittagong in the east.
- He was called a *'Darvesh'*or a *'Zinda Pir'*. He also forbade *Sati.*
- The empire lost power after Aurangzeb's rule. Beacuse his successors were weak and incapable rulers.

THE SURI DYNASTY

Sher Shah Suri (1540 - 1545)

- Founded by Sher Shah Suri ruled in Delhi (North India) from 1540-1555.
- Real name was Farid. Given the title **Sher Khan** by Babar Khan Lohani (Governor of Bihar) who appointed him *Vakil* (deputy)
- After the exit of Humayun, he became the master of Delhi.
- Died in 1545 while campaigning against Kalinjar Fort.
- Introduced the silver 'Rupaya'and the copper 'Dam'and abolished all old and mixed metal currency.
- Built his tomb at Sasaram.
- Built a new city on the bank of Yamuna river (present day *Parana Qila)* at Delhi.
- Malik Mohammad Jaisi composed *Padmavat* (in Hindi) during his reign.

Later Mughals

- **Bahadur Saha I** (1707-1712) Original name was Muazzam; Title-Shah Alam I.
- **Jahandar Shah** (1712-1713) He ascended the throne with the help of Zulfikar Khan; abolished Jaziya.
- **Farruikhsiyar** (1713-1719)
- **Muhammad Shah** (1719-1748) Nadir Shah invaded India and took away Peacock thrown and Kohinoor diamond.
- **Ahmed Shah** (1748-1754) Ahmad Shah Abdali (General of Nadir Shah) marched towards Delhi and the Mughals ceded Punjab and Multan.
- **Alamgir** (1754-1759) Ahmad shah occupied Delhi. Later, Delhi was plundered by Marathas.
- **Shah Alam II** (1759-1806) could not enter Delhi for 12 years.
- **Akbar II** (1806-1837) pensioner of East India Company.
- **Bahadur Shah II** (1837-1857) Last Mughal Emperor who was made premier during the 1857 Revolt.

Literature of Mughal Period

Author	Work
Babar	Tuzuk-i-Babari
Abul Fazal	Ain-i-Akbari, Akbarnamah
Abdul Qadir Badauni	Kitab-ul-Ahadish, Tarikh-i-Alfi, Muntakhab-ul-Tawarkh
Khwaja Nizamuddin Ahmed Harawi	Tabaqat-i-Jahangir
Jahangir	Tuzuk-i-Jahangir
Hamid	Padshahnama
Darashikoh	Majn-ul-Bahrain
Mirza Md Qazim	Alamgirnama

Marathas (AD 1674-1818)

Shivaji (AD 1627-1680)

- Born at Shivner father **Shahji Bhonsle** and mother **Jijabai.** Religious teacher was Samarth Ramdas and guardian was Dadaji Kondadev.
- **Treaty of Purandar** (AD 1665) between Shivaji and Mughals.
- Coronation at Raigarh (AD 1674) and assumed the title of **Haindava Dharmadharak** (Protector of Hinduism).
- **Ashtapradhan** (eight ministers) helped in administration. These were **Peshwas, Sar-i-Naubat** (Military), **Mazumdar or Amatya** (Accounts); **Waqenavis** (Intelligence); **Surunavis** (Correspondence); **Dabir or Sumanta** (Ceremonies); **Nyayadhish** (Justice); and **Panditrao** (Charity).
- Successors of Shivaji were **Shambhaji, Rajaram,** and **Shahu** (fought at Battle of Khed in AD 1708).

Peshwas (AD 1713 - 1718)

- Founded by **Balaji Vishwanath,** became peswa in 1713, who concluded an agreement with the Sayyid Brothers (the king makers in history) by which Mughal emperor Farukh Siyyar recognized Shahu as the king of Swarajya.
- **Baji Rao** considered as the "greatest exponent of guerilla tactics after Shivaji"; Maratha power reached its zenith and system of confederacy begun; defeated Siddis of Janjira; (1722) conquest of Bassein and Salsette from Portuguese (1739).
- **Balaji Baji Rao** known as Nana Sahib; **Third Battle of Panipat** (AD 1761) between Marathas and Ahmad Shah Abdali gave a big jolt to Marathas empire. They battle ended the Maratha power.

Sikh Gurus

- **Nanak** (1469-1539) founder of Sikh religion.
- **Angad** (1538-1552) invented Gurmukhi.
- **Amardas** (1552-1574) struggled against sati system and purdah system and established 22 Gadiyans to propagate religion.
- **Ramdas** (1574-1581) founded Amritsar in 1577. Akbar granted the land.
- **Arjan** (1581-1606) founded **Swaran Mandir** Golden Temple and composed Adi Granth.
- **Hargobind Singh** (1606-1645) established **Akal Takht** and fortified Amritsar.
- **HarRai** (1645-1666)
- **Harkishan** (1661-1664)
- **Tegh Bahadur** (1664-75)
- **Gobind Singh** (1675-1708) was the last Guru who founded the Khalsa. After him Sikh guruship ended.

THE ADVENT OF EUROPEANS

PORTUGUESE

- **Vasco da Gama** reached Calicut on May 17,1498. During the reign of a king Zamorin. In 1502. he established a factory at Cochine.
- The first Governor of Portuguese in India was Francisco Almeida and he was followed by Alfonso d' Albuquerque in 1509, Who gave them new heights. He captured Goa in 1510 from the Bijapur ruler and also abolished *Sati.*

DUTCH

- Dutch East India Company was formed in 1602.
- They set-up their first factory at Masulipatnam in 1605. Their other factories were at Pulicat, Chinsura, Patna, Balasore, Nagapattanam, Cochin, Surat, Karikal, Kasimbazar.
- They replaced the Portuguese, as the most doment power in European trial with the east including India.

ENGLISH

- The English East India Company was formed in 1599, and was given the royal

Charter by Queen Elizabeth 1 in 1600 to trade in the east.

- An imperial *farman* allowed by Jahangir Permitting the Company to set up a permanent factory at Surat in 1613. Sir Thomas Roe played a vital role in this.

FRENCH

- The French East India Company was set in 1664, at the instance of a minister, Colbert, in the reign of Louis XIV.
- They established their first factory at Surat in 1668 and at Masulipatnam in 1669.

Governor-Generals of Bengal

Warren Hastings (AD 1772-1785)

- Brought the **dual government** to an end by the **Regulating Act,** 1773.
- The Act of 1781 was the clear demarcation between the jurisdiction of the Governor General-in-Council and Supreme Court at Calcutta.
- **Pitt's India Act** (1784), Rohilla War (1774), First Maratha War (1775-1782) and Treaty of Salbai with Marathas (1782); Second Mysore War (1780-84).
- Foundation of Asiatic Society of Bengal (1784) in Calcutta by Sir William Jones.
- The translator of **Abhigyan-shakuntlam** in English in 1789 and wrote introduction to the English translations of **Bhagvadgita** by Charles Wilkins.

Sir John Mackfferson - (1785 -1786) - oppointed temporary general governer.

Lord Cornwallis (AD 1786-93)

- The **Third Anglo Mysore War** (1789-92) and Treaty of Seringapatnam (1792).
- Introduced permanent settlement in Bengal and Bihar (1793).
- Called the **Father of Civil Services** in India, introduced judicial reforms by separating revenue administration from judicial administration, and established a system of circles (thanas) headed by a Daroga (an Indian).

Sir John Shore (AD 1793-98)

- **1 charter Act of 1793.**
- **Battle of Kharda** between the Nizams and the Marathas (1795).

Lord Wellesley (AD 1798-1805)

- Introduction of the **Subsidiary Alliance** (1798), first alliance subsidiary was signed with Nizam of Hyderabad followed by Mysore, Tanjore, Awadh, the Peshwa, the Bhonsle and the Scindia.
- **Treaty of Bassein** (1802) and the **Second Maratha War**

George Barlow (AD 1805-1807)

- Muting at vellor in (1806).

Lord Minto I (AD 1807-1813)

- **Treaty of Amritsar** with Maharaja Ranjit Singh (1809).
- **Charter Act of 1813** was passed.

Lord Hasting (AD 1813-23)

- **Gorkha war Anglo Nepal War** (1814-1816) and Treaty of Sagauli (1816).
- **Third Maratha War** (1817-18) dissolution of Maratha confederacy and creation of Bombay Presidency.
- Pindari War (1817 - 1818) and establishment of **Ryotwari System** by Thomas Munro (1820).

Lord Amherst (AD 1823-1828)

- First Burmese War (1824-26), Treaty of Yandaboo (1826) and capture of Bharatpur(1826).

GOVERNOR GENERALS OF INDIA

Lord William Bentinck (1828 -1835)

- Carried out the social reforms like **Prohibition of Sati** (1829) and **elimination of thugs** (1830).
- English was made as the medium of higher education in the country (After the recommendations of *Macaulay).*
- Suppressed child sacrifice and female infanticide.

- Charter Act of 1833 was passed; made him the **first Governor General of India.** The designation was Governor General of Bengal before him.

Sir Charles Metcalfe (1835 -1836)

- Abolished all restrictions on vernacular press (called *Liberator of the* Press).

Lord Auckland (1836 - 1842)

- First Afghan War (1838 - 1842), which proved to be a disaster for the English.

Lord (1842 - 1844)

- Brought an end to the Afghan war (1843). Annexation of Sindh (1843). Abolished slavery (1843)

Lord Hardinge I (1844 - 1848)

- First anglo Sikh-war (1845 - 46) and treaty of Lahor (1846)

Lord Dalhousie (1848 - 1856)

- Opened the first Indian Railway in 1853 (from Bombay to Thane).
- Laid out the telegraph lines in 1853 (First was from Calcutta to Agra).
- Established the postal system on the modern lines through the length and breadth of the country, which made communication easier.
- Introduced the **Doctrine of Lapse** and capturerd Satara (1848), Jaipur and Sambhalpur (1849), Udaipur (1852), Jhansi (1853) and Nagpur (1854).
- Started Engineering college at Roorkee.
- Encouraged science, commerce, mineralogy, forestry and industry.
- In 1854, *'Wood's Dispatch'* was passed, which provided for the properly articulated system of education from the primary school to the university.
- Remarriage of widows was legalized by **Widow Remarriage Act, 1856).** Due to *Ishwar Chandra Vidyasagar's* efforts.

Veceroys of India

Lord Canning (AD 1856-62)

- The **last Governor General** and the **first Viceroy.**
- Revolt of 1857, Mutiny took place.
- The Universities of Calcutta, Bombay and Madras were established in 1857.
- Withdraw Doctrine of Lapse.
- Passed the Act, 1858 which ended the rule of East India Company.
- Indian Penal Code 1859, code of criminal Procedure (1859) and High Court act (1861) were introduced.

Lord Elgin (AD 1862)

- Suppressed Wahabi Movement.

Lord John Lawrence (AD 1864-69)

- Established the **High Courts** at Calcutta, Bombay and Madras in 1865.
- Created the Indian Forest Department.
- Telegraphic communication was opened with Europe.
- Bhutan War (1865)

Lord Mayo (AD 1869-72)

- Started the process of financial decentralization in India.
- Established the Rajkot college at Kathiarwar and Mayo college at Ajmer for the Indian princes.
- Established the Department of Agriculture and Commerce.
- Organised the statistical survey of India and for the **first time** in Indian history, a **Census** was held in 1871.
- He was the only viceroy to be murdered in office by a Pathan convict in the Andamans in 1872.

Lord Northbrook (AD 1872-1876)

- Abolition of income tax.
- Kuka movement in punjab in 1872.

Lord Lytton (AD 1876-80)

- **Royal Titles Act of 1876** and the assumption of the title of 'Empress of India' by Queen Victoria, the Delhi Durbar in January 1877.
- **Vernacular Press Act** and the **Arms Act** (made it mandatory for Indians to acquires license in arms) of 1878.
- The second Afghan war (1878-80)

Lord Ripon (AD 1880-84)

- **First Factory Act** of 1881. (prohibited labour) first organised census was held in 1882.
- **Local Self-Government** was introduced in 1882.
- Repealed the Vernacular Press Act in 1882.
- Finances of the centre were divided.
- An **Education Commission** was appointed under Sir William Hunter in 1882.
- The **Ilbert Bill Controversy** (1883).

Lord Dufferin (AD 1884-88)

- Establishment of the Indian National Congress in 1885.
- **Third Burmese War** (AD 1885-86).

Lord Lansdowne (AD 1888-94)

- Factory Act of 1891 granted stipulated working hours for women and children and weekly holiday.
- Indian Councils Act of 1892.
- The **Durand Commission** defined the Durand Line between British India and Afghanistan (now between Pakistan and Afghanistan) in 1893.
- Tilak celebrated the Ganpati festival (1893)

Lord Elgin II (AD 1894-99)

- Great famine of 1896-1897 and Lyall Commission on famine was established.
- Southern uprisings of 1899.

Lord Curzon (AD 1899-1905)

- A commission was appointed under Sir Thomas Raleigh in 1902, to suggest reforms regarding universities, the **Indian Universities Act** of 1904 was passed on the basis of its recommendations.
- Ancient Monuments Preservation Act of 1904. Archaeological survey of India was established.
- **Agricultural Research Institute** was established at Pusa in Delhi.
- Partition of Bengal on 16th October 1905.
- Colonel Young Husband's Expedition to Tibet in 1904.

Lord Minto II (AD 1905-1910)

- Swadeshi Movement (1905-08); foundation of Muslim League (1906); Surat Session and split in the Congress (1907).
- News paper act 1908.
- Morley-Minto Reforms (1909).

Lord Hardinge (AD 1910-16)

- Capital shifted from Calcutta to Delhi (1911); Delhi Durbar; Partition of Bengal was reversed in 1911, Gadhar party formed in San toranaslo.
- The Hindu Mahasabha was establesed in 1915 by Pandit Madan Mohan Malaviya.

Lord Chelmsford (AD 1916-21)

- Gandhi returned to India (1915) and founded the **Sabarmati Ashram** (1916), Champaran Satyagraha, Satyagraha at Ahmedabad (1918), Kheda Satyagraha (1918).
- Home rule movement launched by tilak and Annie Basant (1916).
- August Declaration (1917) by Montague, the then Secretary of State, and Montford reforms or the Government of India Act of 1919.
- **Rowlatt Act** (March, 1919) and the **Jallianwala Bagh Massacre** (April 13, 1919).
- Khilafat Movement started, (1919-20).

Non-cooperation Movement started (1920-22).

- Women's University was founded at Poona (1916).

Lord Reading (AD 1921-26)

- Repeal of Press act of 1910 and Row lett act of 1919.
- Moplah Rebellion (1921) took place in Kerala.
- Formation of Swaraj Party (1923).

- Chaura-Chauri Incident (1922).
- Suppressed Non-cooperation Movement.
- **Kakory Train** Robbery on August 1, 1925.
- RSS, founded in 1925.
- **Communal Riots** of 1923-25 in Multan, Amritsar, Delhi etc.

Lord Irwin(AD 1926-31)

- **Simon Commission** announced in 1927.
- Nehru Report (1928).
- Congress passed the Indian Resolution in 1929.
- Lahore Session of Congress and **Poorna Swaraj** Declaration (1929).
- Dandi March (March 12, 1930).
- Civil Disobedience Movement (1930).
- First Round Table Conference was held in England in 1930.
- Gandhi-Irwin Pact (1931).

Lord Willingdon (AD 1931-36)

- **Second Round Table Conference** in London in 1931 and **third** in 1932.
- Fromation of congress social Party - CSP (1934)
- Government of India Act, (1935), Burma separated from India (1935).
- Communal Awards (August 16, 1932) assigned seats to different religious communities. Gandhiji went on a **epic fast** to protest against this division.

Lord Linlithgow (AD 1936 - 43)

- Congress Ministries resignation celebrated as **'Deliverance Day'** by the Muslim League (1939), the Lahore Resolution (March 23, II 1940) of the Muslim League demanding separate state for the Muslims. (It was at this session that Jinnah propounded his Two-Nation Theory).
- Formation of forward black by Subhash Chandra Bose (1939).
- Outbreak of World War II in 1939.
- Cripps Mission in 1942, Quit India Movement (August 8,1942).

Lord Wavell (AD 1943 - 47)

- C.R. furmula 1944.
- Cabinet Mission Plan (May 16, 1946).
- Arranged the **Shimla Conference** on June 25, 1945 with Indian National Congress and Muslim League failed.
- First meeting of the Constituent Assembly was held on December 9, 1946.

Lord Mountbatten (AD March 1947 - August 1947)

- **Last viceroy** of British India and the **first Governor General** of free India.
- Partition of India decided by the June 3, 1947 Plan or Mountbatten Plan.
- Indian Independence Act was passed by the British Parliament on July 4, 1947, by which India became independent on August 15, 1947.
- Retired in June 1948 and was succeeded by **C Rajagopalachari** the first and the last Indian Governor General of Free India.

The Revolt of 1857

Causes of the Revolt

- **Political Causes** The policy of Doctrine of Lapse.
- **Economic Causes** Heavy taxation, evictions, discriminatory tariff policy against Indian products and destruction of traditional handicrafts that hit peasants, artisans and small zamindars .
- **Military Discrimination** Indian soldiers were paid low salaries, they could not rise above the rank of subedar and were racially insulted.
- **Religious Discrimination** The introduction of Enfield rifle, the cartridge of which was geased with animal fat made of Beaf and Pork, provided the spark. British social reforms (widow remarriage (1856), abolition of sati (1829), education for girls, Christians missionaries).

- The Nizam of Hyderabad, the Raja of Jodhpur, Scindia of Gwalior, the Holkar of Indore, the rulers of Patiala, Sindh and Kashmir and the Rana of Nepal provided active support to the British.
- Comparative lack of efficient leadership.

Impact of the Revolt

- The control of Indian administration was passed on to the **British Crown** by the Government of India Act, 1858.
- Doctrine of Lapse was withdrawn.
- Reorganisation of army.
- After the revolt, the British pursued the Policy of **Divide and Rule.**

Chief National Activities

The Indian National Congress (I.N.C)

- It was formed in 1885 by **AO Hume.**
- The first session was held in Bombay under Presidentship of WC Banerjee in 1885, attended by 72 delegates from all over India.
- The first two decade of NC are described in history as those of moderate demands and a sense of confidence in British justice and generosity.
- **Moderate leaders** Dada Bhai Naoroji, Badruddin Tayabji, Gopal Krishna Gokhale, Surendranath Banerjee, Anand Mohan Bose.

Partition of Bengal (1905)

- By **Lord Curzon on** 16 October, 1905 through a royal proclamation, reducing the old province of Bengal in size by creating and east bangel which later on become east Pakistan and present day Banglades.

Swadeshi Movement (1905 - 1908)

- Had its origin in the anti-partition movement of Bengal.
- Lal, Bal, Pal and Aurobindo Ghosh played an important role.
- INC took the swadeshi call first at the Banaras Session, 1905 presided over by GK Gokhale.

Muslim League (1906)

- Setup in Dec. 1906 by Aga Khan, Nawab Salimullah of Dhaka and Nawab Mohsin-ul-Mulk.
- The League supported the partition of Bengal and opposed the Swadeshi Movement, demanded special safeguards to its community and a separate electorate for Muslims. This led to communal differences between Hindus and Muslims.

Demand for Swaraj (Calcutta Session in December 1906)

- The INC under the leadership of Dadabhai Naoroji adopted 'Swaraj' (Self-government) as the goal of Indian People.

Surat Session (1907)

- The INC split into two groups— The extremists and the moderates.
- Extremists were led by Bal, Lal, Pal while the moderates by GK Gokhale.

Minto Morley Reforms (1909)

- The reforms envisaged a separate electorate for Muslims besides other Constitutional measures.

Ghadar Party (1913)

- Formed by Lala Hardayal, Taraknath Das and Sohan Singh Bhakna. Head Quarter—San Francisco.
- The name was taken from a weekly paper, Ghadar, which had been started on November 1, 1913 to commemorate the 1857 Revolt.

Home Rule Movement (1916)

- Started by BG Tilak (April, 1916) at Poona and Annie Besant and S. Subramania lyer at Adyar, near Madras (September, 1916).
- Establishment of two home rule league are main **objective** Self-government for India in the British Empire.
- Tilak supported the movement and joined Annie Besant. He raised the slogan: **Swaraj is my Birth right and I will have it.**

Lucknow Pact Congress league Pact (1916)

- Pact between INC and Muslim league following a war between Britain and Turkey leading to anti-British feelings among Muslims.
- Both organisations jointly demand dominion status for the country.

August Declaration (1917)

- After the Lucknow pact, the British policy was announced which aimed at "increasing association of Indians in every branch of the administration for progressive realization of responsible government in India as an integral part of the British empire". This came to be called the August Declaration.
- The Montague—**Chelmsford reforms** or the Act of 1919 was based on this declaration.

Rowlatt Act (March 18, 1919)

- This gave unbridled powers to the government to arrest and imprison suspects without trail.
- **Satyagrah** was started against this act. This was the first country wide agitation by Gandhiji.

Jallianwala Bagh Massacre (April 13, 1919)

- On April 13,1919 people were protest against the arrest of **Dr Kitchlu** and **Dr Satyapal** under Rowlatt act on April 10, 1919.
- General **O' Dyer** ordered to fire at people who assembled in the Jallianwala Bagh, Amritsar. Hunter Commission was appointed to enquire into it.
- Rabindra Nath Tagore returned his knighthood in protest.
- Sardar **Udham Singh** killed **General Dyer** in Caxton Hall, London in 1940.

Khilafat Movement (1920 - 22)

- Muslims were agitated by the treatment done with Turkey by the British in the treaty that followed the **First World War.**
- Ali brothers, **Mohd Alli** and **Shaukat Ali** started this movement. It was jointly led by the Khilafat leaders and the Congress.

Non-Cooperation Movement (1920)

- Congress passed the resolution in its Calcutta Session in September, 1920.
- It was the first mass-based political movement under Gandhiji.
- Resignation from nominated offices and posts in the local bodies.
- Refusal to attend government *durbars* and boycott of British courts by the lawyers.
- Refusal of general public to offer themselves for military and other government jobs and boycott of foreign goods.

Chauri-Chaura Incident (1922)

- The Congress Session at Allahabad in December 1921. decided to launch a Civil Disobedience Movement. Gandhiji was appointed its leader.
- But before it could be launched, a mob of people at Chauri-Chaura (near Gorakhpur) clashed with the police and burnt 22 police men on February 5, 1922.
- This compelled Gandhiji to withdraw the Non-Cooperation Movement on February 12, 1922.

Simon Commission (1927)

- Constituted by John Simon, to review the political situation in India and to introduce further reforms and extension of parliamentary democracy.
- Indian leaders opposed the Commission, as there were no Indians in it they cried **Simon Go Back.**
- The Government used brutal repression at Lahore, **Lala Lajpat Rai** was beaten in lathi-charge. He succumbed to his injuries on Oct 30, 1928.

The Nehru Report (1928)

- After boycotting the Simon Commission, all political parties constituted a committee under the chairmanship of **Motilal Nehru** and Tej Bahadur Sapru to evolve and determine the principles for the Constitution of India. The report failed.

Lahore Session (1929)

- On December 19, 1929, under the presidentship of J **L Nehru,** the INC, at its Lahore Session, declared **Poorna Swaraj** (Complete Independence) as its ultimate goal.
- The tri-colour flag adopted on December 31, 1929, was unfurled, and January 26, 1930 was fixed as the First Independence Day, to be celebrated every year. Later this day was chosen as the Republic Day of India.

Dandi March/Salt Satyagraha (1930)

- Gandhiji started his march from Sabarmati Ashram on March 12, 1930 for the small village Dandi to break the salt law.
- He picked a handful of salt and inaugurated the **Civil Disobedience Movement.**
- Soon thereafter followed repressive measures such as mass arrests, lathi charge, Police firing etc. about 100,000 people went in jail.
- Countrywide mass participation by women.
- The Garhwal soldiers refused to fire on the people at Peshawar.

First Round Table Conference (1930)

- It was held on November 12, 1930 in London to discuss Simon Commission. It was the first conference arranged between the British and Indians as equals.
- Hindu Mahasabha and Muslim League participated in it. The Conference failed due to absence of INC.

Gandhi Irwin Pact (1931)

- The government represented by Lord Irwin and INC by Gandhiji signed a pact on March 5, 1931.
- In this the INC called off the Civil Disobedience Movement, and agreed to join the Second Round Table Conference.
- The government allowed the villagers on the coast to make salt for consumption and released the political prisoners.
- The Karachi Session of 1931 endorsed the Gandhi Irwin Pact.

Second Round Table Conference (1931)

- Gandhiji represented the INC and went to London to meet British Prime Minister Ramsay MacDonald.
- The conference however failed as Gandhiji could not agree with British Prime Minister on his Policy of communal representation and refusal of the British Government on the basic Indian demand for freedom.

The Communal Award (August 16, 1932)

- Announced by **Ramsay McDonald.** It showed divide and rule policy of the British.
- It envisaged communal representation of depressed class, Sikhs and Muslims.
- Gandhiji opposed it and started fast unto death in Yervada jail.

Poona Pact (September 25, 1932)/Gandhi-Ambedkar Pact

- The idea of separate electorate for the depressed classes was abandoned, but seats reserved for them in the provincial legislature were increased.
- Thus, Poona Pact agreed upon a joint electorate for upper and lower castes.

Third Round Table Conference (1932)

- Proved fruitless as most of the national leaders were in prison.

Demand for Pakistan

- In 1930, Iqbal suggested that North-West Provinces and Kashmir should be made Muslim state within the federation.
- **The term Pakistan** was given by **Chaudhary Rehmat Ali** in 1933.

- Muslim League first passed the proposal of separate Pakistan in its Lahore Session in 1940 (called Jinnah's Two-Nation Theory). It was drafted by Sikandar Hayat Khan, moved by Fazlul Haq and seconded by Khaliquzzamah.
- The Karachi Session of the Muslim League adopted the slogan "Divide and Quit" in December 1943.

August Offer (8 August, 1940)

- It offered (*i*) Dominion status in the unspecified future, (*ii*) A post-war body to enact the Constitution (*iii*) to expand the Governor-General's Executive Council to give full weightage to minority opinion.
- This was accepted by the Muslim League but was rejected by INC.

The Cripps Mission (1942)

- The British government with a view to get co-operation from Indians in 2nd World War, sent Sir **Stafford Cripps** to settle with Indian leaders.
- He offerred dominion status to be grated after war.
- Congress rejected it. Gandhiji termed it as post *dated cheque on a crashing bank.*

The Revolt of 1942 and The Quit India Movement

- Called the **Vardha Proposal** and Leaderless Revolt.
- The resolution was passed on August 8, 1942, at Bombay Gandhiji gave a call for **'Do or Die'** to his countryman.
- On August 9, the congress was banned and its important leaders like Gandhi, Nehru, Patel etc. were arrested. Gandhiji was kept at the Aga Khan Palace, Pune.
- The people became violent. The movement was, however, crushed by the government.

Indian National Army (INA)

- INA was borned by Mazor Mohan Singh.
- **Subhash Chandra Bose** has escaped to Berlin in 1941 and set up an Indian League there. In July 1943, he joined the INA at Singapore. Ras Bihari Bose handed over the leadership to him.
- INA had three fighting brigades names after Gandhi, Subhas and Nehru. Rani of Jhansi Brigade was an exclusive women force.
- INA headquarters at Rangoon and Singapore.

The Cabinet Mission Plan (1946)

- Members, Patrick Lawrence, Alexander, Stafford Cripps.
- Main proposals
  1. Rejection of demand for full fledge Pakistan.
  2. Loose union under a centre with centres control over defence and foreign affairs.
  3. Provinces were to have full autonomy and residual powers.
  4. Provincial legislatures would elect a Constituent Assembly.
- Both Congress and Muslim league accepted it.

Formation of Interim Government (September 2, 1946)

- On 2 September, 1946 in accordance with Cabinet Mission proposals and was headed by **J.L. Nehru.** Muslim League refused to join it initially.

Formation of Constituent Assembly (December, 1946)

- The Constituent Assembly met on December 9, 1946 and Dr Rajendra Prasad was elected as its President.
- Muslim League did not join it.

Jinnah's-Direct Action Resolution (August 16,1946)

- The election result did not favour ML, so Jinnah withdrew his acceptance to Cabinet Mission Plan and Jinnah celeberated Pakistan Day on March 27, 1947.

  ML passed a 'Direct Action' resolution, which condemned both the British Government and the Congress (August 16, 1946).

Mountbatten Plan (June 3, 1947)

The Plan formulated by Lord Mountbatten outlined that

- India to be divided into India and Pakistan.
- A separate Consitutional Assembly for Pakistan to frame its Constitution.
- The liberty to join either India or Pakistan or even remain independent.
- A separate state of Pakistan would be erected.
- Boundary Commission was to be headed by Radcliffe.

Partition and Independence (August 1947)

- Indian Independence Act, 1947 implemented on 15th August 1947, abolished the sovereignty of British Parliament.
- Dominions of **India** and **Pakistan** were created. Each dominion was to have a Governor-General.
- Pakistan was to comprise Sind, British Baluchistan, NWFP, West Punjab and East Bengal.
- There were 562 big and small pricely states in India. At the time of independence .
- **Sardar Vallabhbhai Patel,** the first home minister, integrated all the states by 15 August 1947. Kashmir, Hyderabad, Junagarh, Goa (with Portuguese) and Pondicherry (with French) later acceded to Indian federation.

SOCIAL AND CULTURAL UPRISINGS

Brahmo Samaj

- In 1828 founded by **Raja Ram Mohan Roy**.
- Other important leaders were **Devendranath Tagore** (father of Rabindranath Tagore) and **Keshab Chandra Sen.**
- Criticized Sati Pratha, casteism and advocated widow remarriage.
- He opposed to Sanskrit system of education, because he thought it would keep the country in darkness.

Arya Samaj

- Founded by **Swami Dayanand** (or, **Moolshankar)** in 1875.
- His saying was 'Go *back to the vedas' & 'India for the Indians'*. He disregarded Puranas, idol worship, casteism and untouchability. He defended widow remarriage.
- Dayanand's views were published in his famous work, *Satyarth Prakash.* (Partly in Hindi and partly in Sanskrit) He also wrote *Veda Bhashya Bhumika* and Veda *Bhashya.*

Ramakrishna Mission

- Founded by **Vivekanand** (earlier, Narendranath Dutta) (1863-1902) in 1897, 11 years after the death of his guru Ram Krishna Paramhans.
- In 1893 Vivekanand attended the Parliament of Religion at Chicago.

Veda Samaj

- Called *Brahmo Samaj of South.* Started by **Sridharalu Naidu.**
- He translated books of Brahmo Dharma into Tamil and Telugu.

Servants of India society

- Formed **by Gopal Krishna Gokhale** in 1915.
- It did notable work in providing famine relief and in improving the condition of the tribal.

Theosophical Society

- Founded by Westerners who drew inspiration from Indian thought and culture.
- **Madam H P Blavatsky** laid the foundation of the movement in US in 1875. Later, **Col. M S Olcott** of the US Army joined her.
- It was shifted to India at Adyar (Tamil Nadu) in 1882.
- **Annie Besant** was elected its President in 1907. She founded the *Central Hindu College* in 1898, which became *Banaras Hindu University* in 1916.

IMPORTANT NEWSPAPERS AND JOURNALS OF FREEDOM STRUGGLE ERA

Newspaper/Journal	Founder/Editor
Bengal Gazette (1780)*(India's first newspaper)*	J.K.Hikki
Native Opinion	V.N. Mandalik
Kavivachan Sudha	Bhartendu Harishchandra
Past Goftar *(first newspaper in Gujarati)*	Dadabhai Naoroji
New India *(Weekly)*	Bipin Chandra Pal
Statesman	Robert Knight
Hindu	Vir Raghavacharya and G.S. Aiyar
Sandhya	B.B. Upadhyaya
Vichar Lahiri	Krishnashastri Chiplunkar
Hindu Patriot	Girish Chandra Ghosh (later Harish Chandra Mukherji)
Som Prakash	Ishwar Chandra Vidyasagar
Kesari	B.G. Tilak
Maharatta	B.G. Tilak
Sudharak	G.K. Gokhale
Amrita Bazar Patrika	Sisir Kumar Ghosh and Motilal Ghosh
Vande Mataram	Aurobindo Ghosh
Yugantar	Bhupendranath Datta and Barinder Kumar Ghosh
Bombay Chronicle	Firoze Shah Mehta
Pratap	Ganesh Shankar Vidyarthi
Essays in Indian Economics	M.G.Ranade
Samvad Kaumudi *(Bengali)*	Ram Mohan Roy
Mirat-ul-Akhbar	Ram Mohan Roy *(first Persian newspaper)*
Indian Mirror	Devendra NathTagore
Nav Jeevan	M.K.Gandhi
Young India	M.K.Gandhi
Harijan	M.K.Gandhi
Prabudha Bharat	Swami Vivekananda
Udbodhana .	Swami Vivekananda
Indian Socialist	Shyamji Krishna Verma
Talwar *(in Berlin)*	Birendra Nath Chattopadhyaya
Free Hindustan *(in Vancouver)*	Tarak Nath Das
Hindustan Times	K.M. Pannikar
Hindustan	M.M. Malviya

Newspaper/Journal	Founder/Editor
Mooknayak	B.R.Ambedkar
Comrade	Mohammad Ali
Tahzib-ul-Akhlaq	Sir Syyed Ahmed Khan
AI-Hilal	Abul Kalam Azad
Al-Balagh	Abul Kalam Azad
Independent	Motilal Nehru
Punjabi ‘	Lala Lajpat Rai
New India (Daily)	Annie Besant
Commonweal	Annie Besant
Kranti	Mirajkar, Joglekar, Ghate

IMPORTANT BOOKS OF FREEDOM STRUGGLE ERA

Work	Author
Causes of the Indian Mutiny	Sir Syyed Ahmed Khan
Pakhtoon	Khan Abdul Gnaffar Khan
Problems of the East	Lord Curzon
Economic History of India	R.C. Dutt
Ghulam Giri	Jyotiba Phule
Unhappy India	Lala Lajpat Rai
To all fighters of freedom, Why Socialism?	J.P. Narayan
Pather Panchali	Bibhuti Bhushan Banerji
The Discovery of India	J.L. Nehru
My Indian Years	Lord Hardinge II
Neel Darpan	Dinbandhu Mitra
Hind Swaraj	M.K. Gandhi
Anand Math	Bankim C. Chatterji
Devi Chaudharani	Bankim C. Chatterji

Work	Author
Sftaram	Bankim C. Chatterji
The Indian Struggle	S.C. Bose
The Spirit of Islam	Syyed Ameer Ali
Precepts of Jesus	Ram Mohan Roy
A Gift of Monotheists	Ram Mohan Roy
Satyarth Prakash	Swami Dayanand
Poverty & Un-British Rule in India	Dadabhai Naoroji
A Nation in the Making	S.N. Banerji
The Indian War of Independence	V.D. Savarkar
India Divided	Rajendra Prasad
What Congress and Gandhi have done to the untouchables	B.R. Ambedkar

IMPORTANT BATTLES IN THE INDIAN HISTORY

B.C. 326	Alexander defeated Porus in the Battle of Hydaspas.
261	Ashoka defeated Kalinga in the Kalinga War.
A.D. 1191 1192	First Battle of Tarain in which Prithviraj Chauhan defeated Mohd. Ghori. Second Battle of Tarain in which Mohd. Ghori defeated Prithviraj Chauhan.

1194	Battle of Chandawar in which Mohd. Ghori defeated Jaichandra of Kannauj.
1526	First Battle of Panipat in which Babar defeated Ibrahim Lodhi.
1527	Battle of Khanua in which Babar defeated Rana Sanga.
1529	Battle of Ghaghara in which Babar defeated the Afghans.
1539	Battle of Chausa in which Sher Shah Suri defeated Humayun
1540	Battie of Kannauj (or Bilgram) in which Sher Shah Suri defeated Humayun and forced him to flee.
1556	Second Battle of Panipat in which Bairam Khan (representing Akbar) defeated Hemu.
1565 1576	Battle of Talikota (or Banihatti) in which an alliance of Ahmednagar, Bijapur, Golkunda and Bidar defeated the Vijaynagar empire (represented by Sadasiva). Battle of Haldighati in which Akbar defeated Maharana Pratap.
1615	Mewar submitted to the Mughals. A treaty of peace was signed between Jahangir and Rana Amar Singh of Mewar.
1658	Battle of Dharmatt and Samugarh in which Aurangzeb defeated Dara Shikoh.
1665	Raja Jai Singh defeated Shivaji and the Treaty of Purandar signed.
1737	Battle of Bhopal in which Baji Rao defeated Mohd. Shah.
1739	Battle of Kamal in which Nadir Shah defeated Mohd. Shah.
1757	Battle of Plassey in which the English forces (under Robert Clive) defeated Siraj-ud-daula, the Nawab of Bengal.
1760	Battle of Wandiwash in which the English forces defeated the French forces.
1761	Third Battle of Panipat in which Ahmed Shah Abdali defeated the Marathas.
1764	Battle of Buxar in which the English under Munro defeated the alliance of Nawab Mir Qasim of Bengal, Nawab Shuja-ud-daula of Awadh and Mughal emperor Shah Alam.
1767-69	First Anglo Mysore War in which Hyder Ali defeated the English forces.
1770	Battle of Udgir in which the Marathas defeated the Nizam.
1766-69	First Anglo Maratha War in which the British were defeated.
1780-84	Second Anglo Mysore War. Hyder Ali died during the battle (1782) and the field was taken by his son Tipu Sultan. The war concluded with the Treaty of Mangalore (1784).
1789-92	Third Anglo Mysore War in which Tipu Sultan was defeated The Treaty of Serirangapatnam followed.
1799	Fourth Anglo Mysore War in which Tipu was defeated and killed.
1803-06	Second Angio Maratha War in which the British defeated the Marathas.
1817-19	Third Anglo Maratha War in which the British defeated the Marathas badly.
1824-26	First Anglo Burmese War in which the British defeated the Burmese.
1839-42	First Anglo Afghan War in which the British defeated the Afghan ruler Dost Mohammad.
1845-46	First Anglo Sikh War in which the Sikhs were defeated.
1848-49	Second Anglo Sikh War in which the Sikhs were defeated and Punjab was annexed by the British.
1852	Second Anglo Burmese War in which the British won.
1865	Third Anglo Burmese War in which the British won & annexed Burma.
1868-80	Second Anglo Afghan War in which the English suffered losses.
1919-21	Third Anglo Afghan War in which the English, though victorious, did not benefit from the war.

Popular Quotations	
• *Hey Ram.*	**Mahatma Gandhi**
• *Jai Jawan Jai Kisan.*	**Lal Bahadur Shastri**
• *Truth and non-violence are my Gods.*	**Mahatma Gandhi**
• *Jan Gan Man Adhinayak Jai Hey.*	**Rabindra Nath Tagore**
• *Dilli Chalo.*	**Subhash Chandra Bose**
• *Swarajya is my birth right.*	**Bal Gangadhar Tilak**
• *Aram Haram Hai.*	**Jawaharlal Nehru**
• *Freedom is not worth having if it does not include the freedom to Wake Mistake.*	**Mahatma Gandhi**
• *Hate the sin, love the sinner.*	**Mahatma Gandhi**

Popular Names of Personalities

Popular Name	Personality
• Andhra Kesri	T Prakasam
• Babuji	Jagjiwan Ram
• Bapu	Mahatma Gandhi
• CR	C Rajagopalachari
• Desh Bandhu	Chitranjan Das
• Grand Old man	Dadabhai Naoroji
• Lal, Bal, Pal	Lala Lajpat Rai, Bal Gangadhar Tilak, Bipin Chandra Pal
• Guru ji	MS Golwalker
• Gurudev	Rabindranath Tagore
• Iron Man	Sardar Vallabh Bhai Patel
• Sparrow	Major Rajender Singh
• JP	Jayaprakash Narayan
• Lady with the lamp	Florence Nightingale
• Lion of the Punjab	Lala Lajpat Rai

Popular Name	Personality
• Little Corporal	Napoleon
• Lokmanya	Bal Gangadhar Tilak
• Jawan	Indian soldier
• Mahamanya	Pt Madan Mohan Malaviya
• Man of Blood	Bismark
• Netaji	Subhash Chandra Bose
• Nightingale of India	Sarojini Naidu
• Panditji	Jawaharlal Nehru
• Shastriji	Lal Bahadur Shastri

Crematoriums of Famous Persons

Crematorium	Famous Person
• Raj Ghat	Mahatma Gandhi
• Vijay Ghat	Lal Bahadur Shastri
• Kisan Ghat	Ch Charan Singh
• Veer Bhumi	Rajiv Gandhi
• Ekta Sthal	Giani Zail Singh, Chandra Shekhar
• Uday Bhoomi	K R Narayana
• Shanti Van	Jawaharlal Nehru
• Shakti Sthal	Indira Gandhi
• Abhay Ghat	Morarji Desai
• Samata Sthal	Jagjivan Ram
• Karma Bhumi	Dr Shankar Dayal Sharma
• Mahaprayan Ghat	Dr Rajendra Prasad

Newspapers and Journals

Name	Published by
• Bengal Gazette (1780) (India's first newspaper)	JK Hikki
• Kesari	BG Tilak
• Maharatta	BG Tilak
• Amrita Bazar Patrika	Sisir Kumar Ghosh and Motilal Ghosh
• Vande Mataram	Aurobindo Ghosh
• Rast Goftar	Dadabhai Naoroji
• Yugantar	Bhupendranath Datta and Barinder Kumar Ghosh
• Bombay Chronicle	Firoze Shah Mehta

■ ■

3 GEOGRAPHY

UNIVERSE

- The universe is commonly defined as the totality of everything that exists, including all physical matter and energy, the planets, stars, galaxies and the contents of intergalactic space.
- The study of universe is known as Cosmology.

  Cosmology = cosmos (*universe*) + logos (*science*)

  The universe has no limit.

GALAXY

- There are about 100 billion galaxies (10^{11} galaxies) in the universe, and each galaxy has, on an average, 100 billion stars (10^{11} stars). So, the total number of stars in the universe is 10^{22} stars.
- The Milky Way Galaxy is the home of the Earth and our Solar System. It is spiral in shape.
- Latest known galaxy is the Dwarf Galaxy.
- Origin of the universe is explained by the Big Bang Theory, formulated and proposed by the Belgian astronomer and cosmologist Georges Lemaitre.
- Andromeda is our nearest galaxy.

THE SOLAR SYSTEM

- The solar system consists of the sun, the eight planets and their satellites (or moons), and thousands of other smaller heavenly bodies such as asteroids, comets and meteors.
- The sun is at the centre of the solar system and all these bodies are revolving around it.
- Planets revolve around the sun in elliptical orbit.

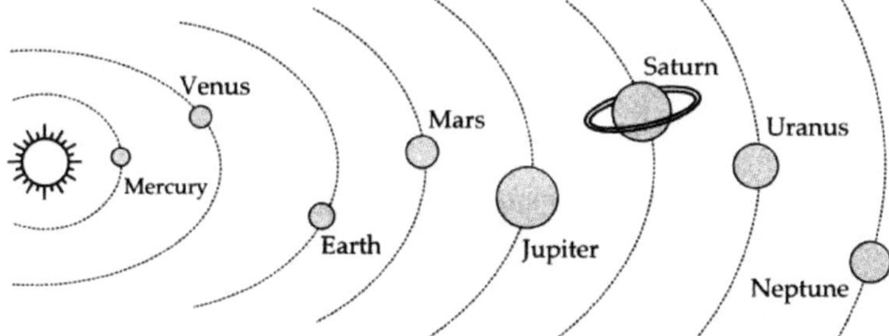

- The sun is also the source of all the energy in the solar system.
- Pluto is a dwarf planet.
- Mercury, Venus, Earth, Mars are called terrestrial planets and Jupiter Saturn, Uranus and Neptune are called gaseous planets.

SOLAR SYSTEM : SOME IMPORTANT FACTS

Biggest Planet	Jupiter	Blue Planet	Earth
Smallest Planet	Mercury	Morning Star	Venus
Nearest Planet to Sun	Mercury	Evening Star	Venus
Farthest Planet from Sun	Neptune	Planet with a Red Spot	Jupiter
Nearest Planet to Earth	Venus	Brightest planet outside Solar System	Sirius (Dog Star)
Brightest Planet	Venus	Closest Star of Solar System	Proxima Centauri
Hottest Planet	Venus	Fastest rotation in Solar System	Jupiter
Coldest Planet	Neptune	Slowest rotation in Solar System	Venus
Red Planet	Mars	Fastest revolution in Solar System	Mercury
Biggest Satellite	Ganymede	Slowest revolution in Solar System	Neptune
Smallest Satellite	Deimos		

SUN : SOME IMPORTANT FACTS

Average distance from Earth	14,95,98,900 km
Diametre	13,91,980 km
Temperature of the Core	1,50,00,000°K
Rotation Speed	25.38 days (with respect to equator): 33 days (with respect to poles)
Chemical composition	Hydrogen : 71%; Helium : 26.5%; Other gases : 2.5%
Age	4.6 billion years
Total life	10 billion years
Time taken by sunlight to reach earth	8 min. and 16.6 sec.
Speed of light (in vaccum)	3,00,000 kmps

EARTH : SOME IMPORTANT FACTS

Age	4,550 million years
Mass	5.976×10^{24} kg
Volume	1.083×10^{24}litres
Mean Density	5.518 kg/lt
Total Surface Area	510 million sq. km
Land Area	29.2% of the total surface area
Water Area	70.8% of the total surface area
Equatorial Diametre	12,755 km
Polar Diametre	12,712 km
Escape Velocity	11.2 km/sec
Highest Land Point	Mount Everest (8,848 m)
Lowest Land Point	Dead Sea (396 m)
Greatest Ocean Depth	Mariana Trench (11,033 m)
Equatorial Circumference	40.076 km
Polar Circumference	40,024 km
Mean Surface Temperature	14°C
Maximum distance from sun (Aphelion)	About 152 million km
Minimum distance from sun (Perihelion)	About 147 million km
Rotation Speed	23 hrs, 56 min & 40.91 sec
Revolution Speed	365 days, 5 hrs & 45.51 sec
Dates when days & nights are equal	Mar. 21 (Vernal Equinox); Sept. 23 {Autumnal Equinox)
Dates of longest days and shortest nights	June 21 (Summer Solstice); Dec. 22 (Winter Solstice)

MOON : SOME IMPORTANT FACTS

Average distance frorn earth	3,84,365 km
Diametre	3,476 km
Ratio of diametre of moon to that of earth	1 : 3.7
Rotation speed	27 days, 7 hrs, 43 min & 11.47 sec.
Revolutïon speed	27 days, 7 hrs, 43 min & 11.47 sec.
Time taken by moonlight to reach earth	1.3 sec
Percent of surface visible from earth	59%
First man to reach moon	Neil Armstrong and Edvin Aldrin on Apollo XI (1969)

WORLD : PHYSICAL FACTS

MAJOR MOUNTAIN RANGES OF THE WORLD

Range	Location	Length (km)
Andes	South America	7,200
Himalayas-Karakoram-Hindukush	South Central Asia	5,000
Rockies	North America	4,800
Great Dividing Range	East Australia	3,600
Atlas	North West Africa	1,930
Western Ghats	Western India	1,610
Caucasus	Europe	1,200
Alaska	USA	1,130
Alps	Europe	1,050

Highest Mountain Peaks of the World

Sl.	Name	Height (in mts.)	Country
1.	Mount Everest	8,848	Nepal
2.	K-2 (Godwin Austin)	8,610	India
3.	Kanchenjunga	8,597	India
4.	Lhotse	8,511	Nepal
5.	Makalu	8,481	Nepal
6.	Dhaulagiri	8,167	Nepal
7.	Manasalu	8,156	Nepal
8.	Choyu	8,153	Nepal
9.	Nanga Parbat	8,125	India
10.	Annapurna	8,091	Nepal

Note : *Top 10 peaks of the world are located in the & Himalayan Range.*

Highest Peaks of Continents

Continent	Peak	Height (in mts.)	Country
Asia	Mt. Everest	8,848	Nepal
S. America	Mt. Aconcagua	6,960	Argentina
N. America	Mt. Mckinley	6,194	Alaska
Africa	Mt. Kilimanjaro	5,895	Tanzania
Europe	Mt. Elbrus	5,663	Russia
Antarctica	Mt. Vinson	5,140	Antarctica
Oceania	Mt. Cook	3,764	New Zealand
Australia	Mt. Kosciuszko	2,230	Australia

Largest Islands of the World

Sl.	Island	Location	Area
1.	Greenland	Arctic Ocean	2,175,600 sq. km
2.	New Guinea	West Pacific	785,753 sq. km
3.	Borneo	Indian Ocean	748,168 sq. km
4.	Madagascar	Indian Ocean	587,713 sq. km
5.	Baffin Island, Canada	Arctic Ocean	503,994 sq. km
6.	Sumatra, Indonesia	Indian Ocean	443,065 sq. km
7.	Great Britain	North Atlantic	229,957 sq. km
8.	Honshu, Japan	Northwest Pacific	225,800 sq. km
9.	Victoria Island, Canada	Arctic Ocean	220,548 sq. km
10.	Ellesmere Island, Canada	Arctic Ocean	183,964 sq. km

Longest Rivers of the World

Sl.	Name	Source	Outflow	Length
1.	Nile	Lake Victoria Africa	Mediterranean Sea	6,690 km
2.	Amazon	Glacier-fed lakes, Peru	Atlantic Ocean	6,296 km
3.	Mississippi-Missouri	Red Rock, Montana (USA)	Gulf of Mexico	6,240 km
4.	Yangtze kiang	Tibetan Plateau, China	China Sea	5,797 km
5.	Ob	Altai Mountains, Russia	Gulf of Ob	5,564 km
6.	Yellow (Huang Ho)	Eastern part of Kunlan Mts., West China	Gulf of Chihli	4,667 km
7.	Yenisel	Tannu-Ola Mts., Western Tuva, Russia	Arctic Ocean	4,506 km
8.	Parana	Confluence of Paranaiba & Grnade rivers, Brazil	Rio de la plata	4,498 km
9.	Irtish	Altai Mountains, Russia	Ob River	4,438 km
10.	Congo	Confluence of Lualaba and Luapula rivers, Zaire	Atlantic Ocean	4,371 km

IMPORTANT CITIES ON RIVER BANKS (WORLD)

City	Country	River
Adelaide	Australia	Torrens
Amsterdam	Netherlands	Amsel
Alexandria	Egypt	Nile
Bangkok	Thailand	Chao Praya
Baghdad	Iraq	Tigris
Berlin	Germany	Spree
Budapest	Hungary	Danube
Chittagong	Bangladesh	Majyani
Canton	China	Si-Kiang
Cairo	Egypt	Nile
Dublin	Ireland	Liffy
Hamburg	Germany	Elbe
Kabul	Afghanistan	Kabul
Karachi ,	Pakistan	Indus
Lahore	Pakistan	Ravi
Leningrad	Russia	Neva
Lisbon	Portugal	Tagus
Liverpool	England	Messey
London	England	Tames
Moscow	Russia	Moskva
Montreal	Canada	St. Lawrence
New Orleans	U.S.A.	Mississipi
New York	U.S.A.	Hudson
Ottawa	Canada	Ottawa
Paris	France	Seine
Philadetphia	U.S.A.	Delaware
Perth	Australia	Swan
Prague	Czech Republic	Vitava
Quebec	Canada	St. Lawrence
Rome	Italy	Tiber
Stalingrad	Russia	Volga
Shanghai	China	Yang-tse-Kiang
Sidney	Australia	Darlling
Saint Luis	U.S.A.	Mississippi
Tokyo	Japan	Arakava
Vienna	Austria	Danube
Warsaw	Poland	Vistula
Washington D. C.	U.S.A.	Potomac
Yangoon	Myanmar	Irrawaddy

Tallest Waterfalls*

Sl.	Waterfall	Location	River	Height (in mts.)
1.	Angel	Venezuela	Tributary of Caroni	979
2.	Tugela	Natal, South Africa	Tugela	948
3.	Tres Hermanas	Peru	—	914
4.	Oloupena	Hawaii, USA	—	900
5.	Vinnufossen	Norway	—	860
6.	Balaifossen	Norway	—	850
7.	Puukaoku	Hawaii, USA	—	840
8.	James Bruce	British Columbia, Canada	—	840
9.	Browne	South Island, New Zealand	—	836
10.	Strupenfossen	Norway	—	820

Some Other Important Waterfalls

1. Victoria falls
   - It is located on Zambezi river in Zambia (Africa) and known as *'the smoke that thunders'*.
2. Jog (Gersoppa) falls.
   - It is the highest fall of India.
   - It is located on river Saravati in Karnataka.
   - The river forms four tracks known as Raja *Rani,* Roarer and *Rocket*

MAJOR LAKES OF THE WORLD

Largest Lake	Caspian Sea	Highest lake	Lake Titicaca
Largest saline water lake	Caspian Sea	Deepest lake	Lake Baikal
Largest fresh water lake	Lake Superior	India's largest lake	Chilka lake

IMPORTANT LAKES OF THE WORLD

Lake	Location	Area (Sq. km.)
Caspian	Russia and CIS	371000
Superior	Canada and USA	82414
Victoria	Tanzania (Africa)	69485
Huron	Canada and USA	59596
Michigan	USA	58016
Tanganyika	Africa	32892
Baikal	Russia (CIS)	31502
Great Bear	Canada	31080
Aral	Russia (CIS)	30700
Great Slave	Canada	28438

CONTINENTS OF THE WORLD

Continents	Area (Sq. km.)	Continents	Area (Sq. km.)
Asia	41667920	Antarctica	14245000
Africa	29800540	Europe	9699550
North America	24320000	Australia	7687120
South America	17599050	–	–

OCEANS OF THE WORLD

Names	Area (Sq. km.)	Greatest Depth
Pacific	166,240000	Mariana Trench
Atlantic	86,560000	Puerto Rico Trench
Indian	73,430000	Java Trench
Arctic	13,230000	—

IMPORTANT DESERTS

Sahara	N. Africa (Includes the Libyan and the Nubian Desert)
Australian	Australia (Includes Gibson, Simpson, Victorian, Great Sandy)
Arabian	Arab Countries {Includes Rub'al Khali & An-Nafad of S.Arabia and Dast-e-Lut & Dast-e-Kavir of Iran)
Kalahari	Africa (mainly in Botswana)
Gobi	Mongolia
Atacama	Central Chile
Patagonian	Argentina
Namib	Namibia
Takla Makan	Sïnkiang, China
Karakum	Turkrnenistan
Sonoran	Arizona and California (USA)
Thar	India

MAJOR GULFS OF THE WORLD

Names	Area (sq. km.)	Names	Area (sq. km.)
Gulf of Mexico	15,44,000	Gulf of St. Lawrence	2,37.000
Gurf of Hudson	12,33,000	Gulf of California	1,62,000
Arabian Gulf	2.38,000	English Channel	89,900

MAJOR PENINSULAS OF THE WORLD

Peninsulas	Areas (sq. km.)	Peninsulas	Area (sq. km.)
Arabia	32,50,000	Labrador	13,00,000
Southern India	20,72,000	Scandinavie	8,00,000
Alaska	15,00,000	Iberian	584,000

ISLANDS

- In decreasing order of size : Greenland, New Guinea, Borneo, Madagaskar, Baffin, etc.
- Largest river island is Majuli (Asom).
- Most populated island is Java (Indonesia).
- Largest island of India is Middle Andaman.

SMALLEST AND BIGGEST COUNTRIES

Smallest Countries in the World

Sl.	Areawise	Populationwise
1.	Vatican City	Vatican City
2.	Monaco	Tuvalu
3.	Nauru	Nauru
4.	Tuvalu	Palau
5.	San Marino	San Marino
6.	Liechtenstein	Monaco
7.	Marshall islands	Liechtenstein
8.	St. Kitts & Nevis	St. Kitts & Nevis
9.	Maldives	Marshall Islands
10.	Malta	Antigua & Barbuda

The Biggest Countries in the World

Sl.	Population wise	% of World population	Areawise
1.	China	19.4%	Russia
2.	India	17.5%	Canada
3.	USA	4.5%	China
4.	Indonesia	3.4%	USA
5.	Brazil	2.8%	Brazil
6.	Pakistan	2.7%	Australia
7.	Bangladesh	2.4%	Argentina
8.	Nigeria	2.3%	Sudan
9.	Russia	2.0%	India
10.	Japan	1.9%	Kazakhstan

FOREIGN TOWNS ASSOCIATED WITH INDUSTRIES

Town (Country)	Associated Industry
Baku (Azerbaijan)	Petroleum
Ship building	Bangkok (Thailand), Belfast (Ireland), Plymouth (England)
Buenos Aires (Argentina)	Meat
Cadiz (Portugal)	Cork
Chicago (U.S.A.)	Agricultural implements, Meat
Cologne (Germany)	Cotton and woollen industries

Town (Country)	Associated Industry
Dhaka (Bangladesh)	Jute
Detroit (U.S.A.)	Motor cars
Dresden (Germany)	Optical and photographic apparatus
Glasgow (Great Britain)	Machinery
Havana (Cuba)	Tobacco, Cigars
Hollywood (U.S.A.)	Film industry
Johannesburg (S. Africa)	Gold mines
Kimberlay (S. Africa)	Diamond mining
Leeds (England)	Woollen goods
Lyons (France)	Silk industries
Manchester (England)	Cotton industry
Mauritius (Indian Ocean)	Fishing, Shipping, Sugar
Milan (Italy)	Silk
Morocco (North Africa)	Leather
Munich (Germany)	Lenses
New Orleans (U.S.A.)	Cotton industry
Osaka (Japan)	Cotton fabrics
Pittsburg (U.S.A.)	Iron and Steel
Sheffield (England)	Cutlery
Venice (Italy)	Glass manufacturing
Vienna (Austria)	Glass manufacturing
Dairy Product	Wellington (New Zealand)

WORLD'S GEOGRAPHICAL SURNAMES

Surname	Name	Surname	Name
Bengal's Sorrow	Damodar River	Key to the Mediterranean	Gibralter
Blue Mountains	Nilgiri Hills	Land of Cakes	Scotland
City of Sky-scrapers	New York	Land of Golden Fleece	Australia
City of Seven Hills	Rome	Land of Maple Leaf	Canada
City of Dreaming Spires	Oxford	Land of Morning Calm	Korea
City of Palaces	Kolkata	Land of Midnight Sun	Norway
City of Golden Gate	San Francisco	Land of the Thousand Lakes	Finland
City of Magnificent Buildings	Washington D.C.	Land of the Thunderbolt	Bhutan
City of Eternal Springs	Quito (S. America)	Land of White Elephant	Thailand
China's Sorrow	Hwang Ho	Land of Five Rivers	Punjab
Cockpit of Europe	Belgium	Land of Thousand Elephants	Laos

Surname	Name	Surname	Name
Dark Continent	Africa	Land of Rising Sun	Japan
Emerald Isle	Ireland	Loneliest Island	Tristan De Gunha (Mid-Atlantic)
Eternal City	Rome	Manchester of Japan	Osaka
Empire City	New York	Pillars of Hercules	Strait of Gibraltar
Forbidden City	Lhasa (Tibet)	Pearl of the Antilles	Cuba
Garden City	Chicago	Playground of Europe	Switzerland
Gate of Tears	Strait of Bab-el-Mandeb	Quaker City	Philadelphia
Gateway of India	Mumbai	Queen of the Adriatic	Venice
Gift of the Nile	Egypt	Roof of the World	The Pamirs, Central Asia
Granite City	Aberdeen (Scotland)	Rose Pink City	Jaipur
Hermit Kingdom	Korea	Sugar bowl of the world	Cuba
Herring Pond	Atlantic Ocean	Venice of the North	Stockholm
Holy Land	Jerusalem	Windy City	Chicago
Island Continent	Australia	Whiteman's grave	Guinea Coast of Africa
Island of Cloves	Zanzibar	Yellow River	Huang Ho (China)
Isle of Pearls	Bahrein (Persian Gulf)		

BIGGEST, HIGHEST, LARGEST, LONGEST IN THE WORLD

Animal, Tallest	Giraffe
Archipelago, Largest	Indonesia
Bird, Fastest	Swift
Bird, Largest	Ostrich
Bird, Smallest	Humming Bird
Bridge. Longest Railway	Huey P. Long Bridge, Louisiana (U.S.A.)
Building, Tallest in the world	Burj, Dubai (UAE)
Canal, Longest Irrïgational	The Kalakumsky canal
Canal, Longest	Suez canal
Capital, Highest	La Paz (Bolivia)
City, Biggest in area	Mount Isa (Australia)
City, Largest in population	Tokyo
City, Costliest	Tokyo
City, Highest	Van Chuan (China)
Continent, Largest	Asia
Continent, Smallest	Australia
Country, Biggest (area)	Russia
Country, Largest (population)	China

Country, Largest (electorate)	India
Creature, Largest	Blue whale
Delta, Largest	Sunderban (Bangladesh & India)
Desert, Largest (World)	Sahara (Africa)
Desert, Largest (Asia)	Gobi
Dam, Largest	Grand Coulee Dam (U.S.A.)
Dam, Highest	Hoover Dam (U.S.A.)
Diamond, Largest	The Cullinan
Dome, Largest	Astrodome, in Housten (U.S.A.)
Epic, Largest	Mahabharat
Irrigation Scheme, Largest	Lloyd Barrage, Sukkhur (Pakistan)
Island, Largest	Greenland
Sea, Largest	Mediterranean sea
Lake, Deepest	Baikal (Siberia)
Lake, Largest (Artificial)	Lake Mead (Boulder Dam)
Lake, Highest	Titicaca (Bolivia)
Lake, Largest (Fresh water)	Superior
Lake, Largest (Salt water)	Caspian
Library, Largest	United States Library of Congress, Washington D.C.
Mountain Peak, Highest	Everest (Nepal)
Mountain Range, Longest	Andes (S. America)
Museum. Largest	British Museum, London
Ocean, Largest	Pacific
Palace, Biggest	Vatican (Italy)
Park, Largest	Yellow Stone National Park (U.S.A.)
Peninsula, Largest	Arabia
Place, Coldest (Habitated)	Verkhoyansk (Siberia)
Place. Dryest	Iqique (in Atacama Desert. Chile)
Place, Hottest	Azizia (Libya. Africa)
Place, Ramiest	Mausinram (Meghalaya. India)
Planet, Biggest	Jupiter
Planet, Brightest	Venus
Planet, Smallest	Mercury
Plateau, Highest	Pamir (Tibet)
Platform, Longest	Kharagpur (India)
Railway, Longest	Trans-Siberian railway
Railway Station, Largest	Grand Central Terminal, Chicago (U.S.A.)
River, Longest	Nile (Africa)
River, Largest	Amazon (S. America)
Sea-bird, Largest	Albatross
Star, Brightest	Sirius

Statue, Tallest	Statue of Motherland, Volgagrad (Russia)
Telescope, Largest Radio	New Mexico (U.S A.)
Tramway, World's first	New Vork
Tunnel, Longest (Railway)	Tanna (Japan)
Tunnel, Longest (road)	Mont Blanc Tunnel between France and Italy
Volcano, Highest	Ojos del Salado (Andes, Ecuador)
Volcano, Most Active	Maunaloa (Hawaii-U.S.A.)
Wall, Longest	Great Wall of China
Waterfall, Highest	Angel (Venezuela)
Water, Lowest body	Dead Sea
Zoo, Largest	Kruger National Park, South Africa

CHIEF AGRICULTURAL PRODUCERS

Rice	China, India, Indonesia, Bangladesh
Wheat	China, India, USA, Russia
Maize	USA, China, Brazil, Mexico
Tea	India, China, Sri Lanka
Cotton	China, USA, India, Pakistan
Rubber	Indonesia, Thailand, Malaysia. India
Coffee	Brazil, Columbia
Coarse Grain	USA, China, India, Romaina

WORLD MINERAL PRODUCTION

Iron Ore	China, Japan, Russia
Copper Ore	Chili, USA, Indonesia
Tin	China, Indonesia, Peru
Lead	China, Australia, USA
Zinc	China, Australia, Peru
Manganese	South Africa, Brazil, Australia
Aluminium	China, Russia, Canada
Cement	China, India, USA
Petroleum	Saudi Arabia, Russia, USA
Natural Gas	Russia, USA, Canada
Silver	Peru, Mexico, China
Coal	China. USA. India

IMPORTANT INDUSTRIES OF THE WORLD

Cotton	China, India, USA
Iron and Steel	China, Japan, USA
Automobile	USA, Japan
Aircraft	USA, UK
Shipbuilding	Japan, USA, South Korea

IMPORTANT BOUNDARIES

Important International Boundary Lines

Sl.	Boundary line	Countries
1.	Durand Line (drawn in 1896)	Pakistan and Afghanistan
2.	Radcliff Line (drawn in 1947)	India and Pakistan
3.	Mc.Mohan Line (drawn in 1914)	India and China (Arunachal Pradesh Region)
4.	24th Parallel	Pakistan claims that it is boundary between India and Pakistan in Rann of Katchh.
5.	17th Parallel	North Vietnam and South Vietnam
6.	38th Parallel	North Korea and South Korea
7.	49th Parallel	Canada and USA
8.	Hiddenberg Line	Germany and Poland
9.	Maginot Line	Germany and France
10.	Seigfried Line	Fortification between Germany and France

INDIA : GEOGRAPHICAL EXTREMES

S.N.	Feature	Description
1.	Area	3.28 million km^2, which is 2.4% of the world's total area
2.	Length (N-S)	3214 kms
3.	Width (E-W)	2933 kms
4.	Length of Land Frontier	15200 kms
5.	Length of Coast Line	7516.6 kms
6.	Latitudinal Extent (mainland)	8° 4′ N to 37° 6′ N
7.	Longitudinal Extent	68° 7′ E to 97° 25′ E
8.	Southern-most Point of Indian Midland	8° 4′ N, known as Kanyakumari or Cape Camorin
9.	Southern-most Point of India	6½°N, known as Indira point or Pugmallion point in Great Nicobar
10.	Highest Peak	Mt. K-2 known as Godwin Austin or Qagir (8611 m)
11.	Highest Dam	Bhakra (226m) on river Satluj in Punjab
12.	Highest Waterfall	Jog (Gersoppa) falls on river Saravati in Karnataka.
13.	Longest River	Ganga (2525 kms)
14.	Longest Dam	Hirakund on Mahanadi river in Odisha
15.	Longest Coast Line	Gujarat coast followed by Andhra coast
16.	Longest Canal	Indira Gandhi canal also called Rajasthan canal
17.	Longest Beach	Marina beach in Chennai
18.	Coldest Place	Drass in J&K (– 45°C)
19.	Hottest Place	Briyawali in Bikaner district of Rajasthan (56°C)
20.	Wettest Place	Mawsynram in Meghalaya (1220 cms/year) ;
21.	Largest Plateau	Deccan plateau
22.	Largest Riverine Island	Majuli island in river Brahmaputra in Assam
23.	Indian Standard Meridian	821/2° E longitude, which passes through Naini near Allahabad
24.	Tropic of Cancer	231/2° N latitude, which passes through 8 states: viz. Gujarat,Rajasthan, Madhya Pcadesh, Chhattisgarh, Jharkhand, West Bengal, Tripura & Mizoram.
25.	Active Volcano	Barren Island in Andaman and Nicobar

IMPORTANT PASSES IN MIDDLE HIMALAYA

Pass	Location	Connectivity
Pirpanjal pass	J&K	Jammu-Srinagar road passes from this pass.
Banihal pass	J&K	Jammu-Srinagar NH-1A passes from this pass. Jawahar tunnel (India's longest road tunnel) is situated on this pass.
Rohtang pass	HP	Kullu-Keylang road passes from this pass.

IMPORTANT PASSES IN INNER HIMALAYA

SI.	Area	Location	Connectivity
1.	Karakoram pass	J&K	India to China
2.	Burzil pass	J&K	Kashmir valley to Central Asia
3.	Zojila pass	J&K	Srinagar to Leh
4.	Bara Lacha-la pass	Himachal Pradesh	Mandi to Leh
5.	Shipki-la-pass	Himachal Pradesh	Shimla to Garetok (Tibbet)
6.	Mana pass	Uttarakhand	Entry to Mansarovar Lake through Kailash Ghati
7.	Niti pass	Uttarakhand	Entry to Mansarovar Lake through Kailash Ghati
8.	Lipulekh pass	Uttarakhand	Entry to Mansarovar Lake through Kailash Ghati
9	Nathu-la-pass	Sikkim	Entry to Chumbi Valley
10.	Jelep-la pass	Sikkim	Kalingpang (West Bengal) to Lhasa (Tibet)
11.	Bomdi-la pass	Ar. Pradesh	__________
12.	Yang-yap pass	Ar. Pradesh	Entry of Brahmaputra river
13.	Pangsad pass	Ar. Pradesh	Dibrugarh to Myanmar

• IMPORTANT PASSES IN SOUTH INDIA

Pass	Location	Connectivity
Bhorghat	Maharashtra	Bombay -Pune
Thalghat	Maharashtra	Bombay-Nasik
Palghat	Kerala	Palkhad - Coimbatore
Shenkota pass	Kerala	Kollam - Madurai

• INDIAN STATES ON INTERNATIONAL BOUNDARIES

Bordering Pakistan	Jammu and Kashmir, Punjab, Rajasthan, Gujarat.
Bordering China	Jammu and Kashmir, Himachal Pradesh, Uttarakhand, Sikkim, Arunachal Pradesh.
Bordering Nepal	Bihar, Uttarakhand, UP, Sikkim, West Bengal.
Bordering Bangladesh	West Bengal, Mizoram. Meghalaya, Tripura, Assam.
Bordering Bhutan	West Bengal, Sikkim, Arunachal Pradesh, Assam.
Bordering Myanmar	Arunachal Pradesh, Nagaland, Manipur, Mizoram.
Bordering Afghanistan	Jammu and Kashmir (Pakistan-occupied area)

• IMPORTANT RIVERS OF INDIA

Name	Origin from	Falls into	Length (km)
Ganges	Combined Sources	Bay of Bengal	2525
Satluj	Mansarovar Rakas Lakes	Chenab	1050
Indus	Near Mansarovar Lake	Arabian Sea	2880
Ravi	Kullu Hills near Rohtang Pass	Chenab	720
Beas	Near Rohtang Pass	Satluj	470
Jhelum	Verinag in Kashmir	Chenab	725
Yamuna	Yamunotri	Ganga	1375
Chambal	M.P.	Yamuna	1050
Ghaghra	Matsatung Glacier	Ganga	1080
Kosi	Near Gosain Dham Peak	Ganga	730
Betwa	Vindhyanchal	Yamuna	480
Son	Amarkantak	Ganga	780
Brahmaputra	Near Mansarovar Lake	Bay of Bengal	2900
Narmada	Amarkantak	Gulf of Khambat	1057
Tapti	Betul Distt in M.P.	Gulf of Khambat	724
Mahanadi	Raipur Distt. in Chhattisgarh	Bay of Bengal	858
Luni	Aravallis	Rann of Kuchchh	450
Ghaggar	Himalayas	Near Fatehabad	494
Sabarmati	Aravallis	Gulf of Khambat	416
Krishna	Western Ghats	Bay of Bengal	1327
Godavari	Nasik distt. in Maharashtra	Bay of Bengal	1465
Cauvery	Brahmagir Range of Western	Ghats Bay of Bengal	805
Tungabhadra	Western Ghats	Krishna river	640

• IMPORTANT INDIAN TOWNS ON RIVERS

Town	River	Town	River
Allahabad	At the confluence of the Ganga & Yamuna	Kota	Chambal
Patna	Ganga	Jabalpur	Narmada
Varanasi	Ganga	Panji	Mandavi
Kanpur	Ganga	Ujjain	Kshipra
Haridwar	Ganga	Surat	Tapti
Badrinath	Alaknanda	Jamshedpur	Swarnarekha
Agra	Yamuna	Dibrugarh	Brahmaputra
Delhi	Yamuna	Guwahati	Brahmaputra
Mathura	Yamuna	Kolkata	Hooghly
Ferozpur	Satluj	Sambalpur	Mahanadi
Ludhiana	Satluj	Cuttack	Mahanadi
Srinagar	Jhalum	Srirangapatna	Kaveri
Lucknow	Gomti	Hyderabad	Musi
Jaunpur	Gomti	Nasik	Godavari
Ayodhya	Saryu	Vijayvada	Krishna
Bareilly	Ram Ganga	Curnool	Tungabhadra
Ahmedabad	Sabarmati	Tiruchirapali	Cauvery

• MAJOR PORTS IN INDIA

Western Coast	Eastern Coast
Kandla (child of partition)	Kolkata-Haldia (riverine port)
Mumbai (busiest and biggest)	Paradip (exports raw iron to Japan)
Jawahar Lal Nehru (fastest growing)	Vishakhapatnam (deepest port)
Marmugao (naval base also)	Chennai (oldest and artificial)
Mangalore (exports Kudremukh iron-ore)	Ennore (most modern-in private hands)
Cochin (natural harbour)	Tuticorin (southernmost) Port Blair (Strategically important)

THE LARGEST STATES (2011)

S.N.	Population wise	Area wise
1.	Uttar Pradesh	Rajasthan
2.	Maharashtra	Madhya Pradesh
3.	Bihar	Maharashtra
4.	West Bengal	Andhra Pradesh
5.	Andhra Pradesh	Uttar Pradesh

THE SMALLEST STATES (2011)

S.N.	Population wise	Area wise
1.	Sikkim	Goa
2.	Mizoram	Sikkim
3.	Arunachal Pradesh	Tripura
4.	Goa	Nagaland
5.	Nagaland	Mizoram

IMPORTANT NATIONAL HIGHWAYS

National Highways	Connectivity
NH-1	Delhi to Amritsar (via Ambala and Jalandhar)
NH-1 A	Jalandhar to Uri (via Madhavpur, Jammu, Srinagar and Baramula)
NH-2	Delhi to Kolkata (via Mathura and Varanasi)
NH-3	Agra to Mumbai (via Gwalior, Indore & Nasik)
NH-4	Mumbai to Chennai (via Pune, Belgaum, Hubli, Bangalore and Ranipet)
NH-5	Behragoda to Chennai (via Cuttack, Vishakhapatnam and Vijaywada)
NH-6	Hazira to Kolkata (via Nagpur, Raipur and Sambalpur Dhule)
NH-7	Varanasi to Kanyakumari (via Nagpur, Bangalore and Madurai)
NH-8	Delhi to Mumbai (via Jaipur, Ahmedabad and Vadodara)
NH-9	Pune to Machilipatnam(via Sholapur and Hyderabad, Vijaywada
NH-10	Delhi to Fazilka proceeding to Indo-Pak border
➤ **NH-7** is the longest National Highway of India.	

IMPORTANT NATIONAL PARKS AND SANCTUARIES OF INDIA

Sl.	Name and Location	Important Species
1.	Kanha National park, Mandla and Balaghat (MP)	Chital, gaur, nilgai, sambar, barasingha. tiger
2.	kaziranga National Park, Jorhat (Assam)	One-horned rhinoceros, elephant, wild buffalo, wild bear, tiger, leopard.
3.	Kinnersani Sanctuary, Khammam (AP)	Chital, tiger, gaur, wolf, nilgai.
4.	Manas Sanctuary, Barpeta (Assam)	One-horned rhinoceros, gaur, elephant, wild buffalo.
5.	Namdapha Sanctuary, Tirap (Ar. Pradesh)	Elephant, Tiger, panther, wild buffalo.
6.	Pachmarhi Sanctuary, Hoshangabad (MP)	Barking deer, bison, bear, tiger.
7.	Palamau Sanctuary, Daltonganj (Jharkhand)	Barking deer, gaur, chital, elephant, panther.
8.	Periyar Sanctuary, Idukki (Kerala)	Elephant, chital, nilgai.
9.	Rohla National Park, Kullu (Himachal Pradesh)	Brown bear, musk deer, snow leopard, snow pigeon, snow cock.
10.	Simlipal Sanctuary, Mayurbhanj (Orissa)	Elephant, gaur, chital, tiger, flying squirrel.
11.	Tadoba National Park, Chandrapur (Mah.)	Chital, chinkara, panther, tiger, sloth bear, gaur.
12.	Wild Ass Sanctuary, Little Rann of Kutchch, (Guj.)	Wild ass, wolf, nilgai, chinkara.
13.	Bandipur National Park, Mysore (karnataka)	Chital, elephant, panther, barking deer, four-horned antelope.
14.	Bhimbandh Sanctuary, Monghyr (Bihar)	Leopard, tiger, wild boar, wolf.
15.	Chandraprabha Sanctuary, Varanasi (UP)	Tiger, Panther, sambar, sloth bear, peafowl.
16.	Corbett National Park, Garhwal (Uttarakhand)	Four horned antelope, elephant, tiger panther, sambar.
17.	Dampa Sanctuary, Aizawl (Mizoram)	Barking deer, Himalayan bear, tiger, elephant.
18.	Dudhwa National Park, Lakhimpur Kheri (UP)	Barking deer, chital, sloth beer, tiger, panther.
19.	Ghandhi Sagar Sanctuary, Mandsaur (MP)	Barking deer, chinkara, chital.
20.	Ghana Bird Sanctuary, Bharatpur (Rajasthan)	Black-buck, sambar, wild boar, chital.
21.	Gir National Park, Junagarh (Gujarat)	Asiatic lion, panther, chital, nilgai, four-horned antelope.
22.	Hazaribagh Sanctuary, Hazaribagh (Jharkhand)	Chital, nilgai, sambar, tiger.

• IMPORTANT CROPS OF INDIA

Rice	West Bengal, Punjab, UP
Wheat	UP, Punjab, Haryana
Maize	Madhya Pradesh, Andhra Pradesh, Karnataka
Bajra	Rajasthan, Gujarat, Maharashtra
Jowar	Maharashtra, Karnataka, MP, AP

TOTAL PULSES	UP, MP, Punjab
TOTAL FOOD GRAINS	UP, Punjab, West Bengal
Groundnut	Gujarat, Tamil Nadu, Andhra Pradesh
Rapeseed And Mustard	Rajasthan, UP, Haryana
Soyabean	Madhya Pradesh, Maharashtra, Rajasthan
Sunflower	Karnataka, Andhra Pradesh, Maharashtra
TOTAL OIL SEEDS	MP, Maharashtra, Rajasthan
Sugarcane	UP, Maharashtra, Karnataka
Cotton	Maharashtra, Gujarat, Andhra Pradesh
Jute and Mesta	WB, Bihar, Assam
Tea	Assam, West Bengal, Himachal Pradesh
Coffee	Karnataka, Kerala, Tamil Nadu
Rubber	Kerala, Tamil Nadu, Karnataka
Silk	Karnataka, Jammu and Kashmir, Andhra Pradesh. In India all 4 varieties of silk are available: Mulberry, tussareri and muga. Mulberry is the main variety, while tussar is mainly found in Bihar.
Tobacco	Gujarat, Andhra Pradesh, Karnataka

AGRICULTURE REVOLUTIONS

REVOLUTION NAME **PRODUCTS**

(*i*) Blue Revolution .... Fisheries
(*ii*) Brown Revolution .... Leather
(*iii*) Gray Revolution .... Housing Development
(*iv*) Green Revolution.. Agriculture
(*v*) Pink Revolution .... Drugs and Pharmaceuticals
(*vi*) Silver Revolution .... Egg Production
(*vii*) White Revolution .... Dairy Development
(*viii*) Yellow Revolution .... Oil seed
(*ix*) Black Revolution .... Petroleum
(*x*) Golden Fiber Revolution .... Jute
(*xi*) Golden Revolution .... Horticulture
(*xii*) Grey Revolution .... Fertilizer
(*xiii*) Red Revolution .... Meat & Tomato Production
(*xiv*) Round Revolution .... Potato
(*xv*) Silver Fiber Revolution .... cotton
(*xvi*) Silver Revolution .... Egg/Poultry
(*xvii*) Evergreen Revolution .... Over all agriculture Development

• IMPORTANT RIVER VALLEY PROJECTS

Bhakhra Nangal Project	On Satluj in Punjab. Highest in India. Ht 226 m. Reservoir is called Gobind Sagar Lake.
Mandi Project	On Beas in HP.
Chambal Valley Project	On Chambal in MP & Rajasthan, 3 dams are there : Gandhi Sagar Dam, Rana Pratap Sagar Dam and Jawahar Sagar Dam.
Damodar Valley Project	On Damodar in Bihar. Based on Tennessee Valley Project, USA.
Hirakund Project	On Mahanadi in Orissa World's longest dam: 4801m
Rthand Project	On Son in Mirzapur, Reservoir is called Govind Vallabh Pant reservoir.
Kosi Proied	On Kosi in N.Sihar.
Mayurkashi Project	On Mayurkashi in WB.
Kakrap Rra Project	On Tapi in Gujarat.
Kizamsagar Project	On Manjra in AP
Nagerjuna Sagar Project	On Krishna in AP
Tungabhadra Project	On Tungabhadra AP and Kamataka.
Shivasamudram Project	On Cauvery in Karnataka. it is the oldest river valley project of India.
Tata Hydel Scneme	Or, Shima in Maharasnlra
Sharavathi Hydel Project	On Jog Falls in Kamataka
Kundah & Periyar Project	In TN.
Farakha Project	On Ganga in WB. Apart power and irrigation it helps to remove silt for easy navigation
Ukal Project	On Tapti in Gujarat.
Mahl Project	On Maht in Gujarat.
Salal Project	On Cnenab in J&K.
Mata Tila Multipurpose Project	On Betwa in UP & MP.
Thein Project	On Ravi, Punjab.
Pong Dam	On Beas Punjab.
Tehri Project	On Bhgirathi, UttaraKhand
Sardar Sarovar Project	On Narmada, Gujarat/MP.

• NICK NAMES OF IMPORTANT INDIAN PLACES

Nick Name	Place	Nick Name	Place
Golden city	Amritsar	Sorrow of Bengal	Damodar river
Manchester of India	Ahmedabad	Sorrow of Bihar	Kosi river
City of seven islands	Mumbai	Blue Mountains	Nilgiri
Queen of Arabian sea	Kochi	Queen of the Mountains	Mussoorie (Uttarakhand)
Space city	Bangaluru	Sacred river	Ganga
Garden City of India	Bangaluru	Hollywood of India	Mumbai
Silicon valley of India	Bangaluru	City of Castles	Kolkata
Electronic city of India	Bangaluru	State of five rivers	Punjab
Pink city	Jaipur	City weavers	Panipat
Gateway of India	Mumbai	City of lakes	Srinagar
Twin city	Hyderabad-Sikandrabad	Steel city of India	Jamshedpur (Called Tatanagar)
City of festivals	Madurai	City of temples	Varanasi
Deccan Queen	Pune		
City of buildings	Kolkata	Manchester of the north	Kanpur
Dakshin Ganga	Godavari	City at Rallies	New Delhi
Old Ganga	Godavari	Heaven of India	Jammu & Kashmir
Egg bowls of Asia	Andhra Pradesh	Boston of India	Ahmedabad
Soya region	Madhya Pradesh	Garden of spices ofIndia	Kerala
Manchester of the South	Coimbator	Switzerland of India	Kashmir
City of Nawabs	Lucknow	Abode of the God	Prayag (Allahabad)
Venice of the east	Kochi	Pittsburg of India	Jamshedpur

• LARGEST, LONGEST, HIGHEST AND SMALLEST IN INDIA

Longest river	Ganges
The longest tributary river of India	Yamuna
The longest river of the south	Godavari
Highest mountain peak	Godwin Austin (K_2)
Largest lake (Fresh water)	Wular lake (Kashmir)
Highest Dam	Bhakhra Dam (Punjab)
Largest Mosque	Jama Masjid, Delhi
Longest Road	Grand Trunk Road
State with longest coastline	Gujarat
Longest railway route	From Jammu to Kanyakumari
Longest tunnel	Jawahar tunnel (Jammu & Kashmir)
Longest national highway	NH-7 which runs from Varanasi to Kanyakumari
Longest Dam	Hirakund Dam (Orissa)
Longest Bridge	PVNR Expressway, Hyderabad (11,600 m)

Longest River Bridge	Mahatma Gandhi Setu, Patna
Largest populated City	Mumbai (1.60 crore)
Largest Museum	National Museum, Kolkata
Largest Delta	Sunderban Delta, W. Bengal
Largest Dome	Gol Gumbaz, Bijapur (Karnataka)
Largest Zoo	Zoological Gardens. Alipur, Kolkata
Largest man-made Lake	Nagarjuna Sagar Dam
Largest Desert	Thar (Rajasthan)
Highest Tower	Pitampura Tower, Delhi
Smallest State (Area)	Goa
Smallest State (Population)	Sikkim
Highest Waterfall	Gersoppa waterfall (Karnataka)
Longest Electric railway line	From Delhi to Koikata via Patna
Densest populated State	West Bengal
Largest cave temple	Kailash temple. Eliora (Maharashtra)
Largest animal Fair	Sonepur (Bihar)
Highest Gateway	Buland Darwaza, Fatehpur Sikri (Agra)
Biggest Hotel	Oberal-Sheraton (Mumbai)
Largest State (Area)	Rajasthan
Largest State (Population)	Uttar Pradesh
Place of heaviest rainfall	Mausinram (Meghalaya)
Largest corridor	Rameshwaram temple coridor (Tamil Nadu)
Largest cantilever span bridge	Howrah Bridge (Kolkata)
Largest forest state	M.P.
Highest straight gravity Dam	Bhakhra Dam
Longest Railway Platform	Kharagpur (W. Bengal)
Largest Stadium	Salt lake (Yuva Bharti), Kolkata
Largest Port	Mumbai
Highest Lake	Devatal (Garhwal)
Largest Lake (Saline water)	Chilka lake, Orissa
Highest Award	Bharat Ratna
Highest Gallantry Award	Paramveer Chakra
Largest Gurudwara	Golden Temple, Amritsar
Deepest river valley	Bhagirathi & Alaknanda

State with longest coastline of South India	Andhra Pradesh
Longest river which forms estuary	Narmada
Largest Church	Saint Cathedral (Goa)
Longest Beach	Marina Beach, Chennai
Highest Battle field	Siachin Glacier
Highest Airport	Leh (Laddakh)
Largest river island	Majuli (Brahmaputra river, Assam)
Largest Planetarium	Birla Planetarium (Kolkata)

RAILWAY ZONES

Sl. No.	Name	Abbr.	Date Established	Route KMs	Headquarters
1.	Central	CR	1951-11-05	3905	Mumbai
2.	East Central	ECR	2002-10-01	3628	Hajipur
3.	East Coast	ECoR	2003-04-01	2572	Bhubaneshwar
4.	Eastern	ER	1952-04	2414	Kolkata
5.	North Central	NCR	2003-04-01	3151	Allahabad
6.	North Eastern	NER	1952	3667	Gorakhpur
7.	North Western	NWR	2002-10-01	5459	Jaipur
8.	North-east Frontier	NFR	1958-01-15	3907	Guwahati

Sl. No.	Name	Abbr.	Date Established	Route KMs	Head-quarters
9.	Northern	NR	1952-04-14	6968	Delhi
10.	South Central	SCR	1966-10-02	5803	Secundera-bad
11.	South East	SECR	2003-04-01	2447	Bilaspur
12.	South Eastern	SER	1955	2631	Kolkata
13.	South Western	SWR	2003-04-01	3177	Hubli
14.	Southern	SR	1951-04-14	5098	Chennai
15.	West Central	WCR	2003-04-01	2965	Jabalpur
16.	Western	WR	1951-11-05	6182	Mumbai
17.	Kolkata Metro	KMR	2010	39.67 Km (25 k_m Line-1 and 14.67 k_m Line-2)	Kolkata

■■

INDIAN POLITY

- The present Constitution was framed by the **Constituent Assembly of India** setup under Cabinet Mission Plan of May 16, 1946.

COMPOSITION OF CONSTITUENT ASSEMBLY

- It was finally passed and accepted on Nov 26, 1949. The last session of the Assembly was held on Jan 24, 1950, which unanimously elected Dr. Rajendra Prasad as the President of India. In all, 284 members of the Assembly signed the official copies of the Indian Constitution which came into effect on Jan 26, 1950, known and celebrated as the **Republic Day of India.**
- Although Constitution was ready on Nov 26, 1949 but was delayed till Jan 26, 1950 because in 1929 on this day Indian National Congress demanded '*Poorna Swaraj' in* Lahore session under J.L. Nehru. [Some of the provisions as those related to *citizenship, elections, provisional Parliament etc,* were given immediate effect].
- Constituent Assembly took 2 years-11 months-18 days to complete the Constitution.
- Originally it had 395 articles & 8 schedules (12 at present).
- Constituent Assembly adopted our National Flag on July 22, 1947. It was designed by Pingali Venkaiah of Andhra- Pradesh.
- The idea to have Constitution was given by M.N. Roy (Political Philosopher).

PREAMBLE TO THE CONSTITUTION

- It is a preface or the introduction to the Constitution. It is not an integral part of Constitution. The interpretation of Constitution is based on the spirit of Preamble.
- The 'Objective Resolution', proposed by Pandit Nehru and passed by the Constituent Assembly, ultimately became the Preamble.
- Idea of preamble borrowed from Constitution of US.
- The words '*SOCIALIST*', '*SECULAR*' and '*UNIT*'Y & '*INTEGRITY*' were added by the 42nd Amendment in 1976.
- Preamble is not justiciable.

FRAMING OF CONSTITUTION OF INDIA

- The Constituent Assembly was set up in November 1946 as per the Cabinet Mission Plan of 1946.
- The members were elected indirectly by the Provincial Assemblies in the ratio of one member per million population.
- There were a total of 389 members in the Constituent Assembly, of which 296 were elected by the members of the Provincial Assemblies and the rest were nominated by the Princely States.

- Its first meeting was held on 9th **December 1946** with **Sachidanand Sinha** as the Interim President. He was the oldest member of the assembly and was elected as Interim President following the French practice. Later, on December 11, 1946 Rajendra Prasad and H.C. Mukherjee were elected as the President and Vice-President of the Assembly respectively. Sir B.N. Rao was appointed as the Constitutional advisor to the Assembly.
- Jawaharlal Nehru moved the objectives resolution in the Assembly on December 13, 1946. It was adopted by the Assembly on January 22, 1947. The Constituent Assembly formed committees for framing the Constitution. Chairman of some important committees are given below.

  Drafting Committee of Constituent Assembly was the most important committee among all the committees. It was set up on 29th August 1947. It consisted total 7 members including chairman.

  1. B.R. Ambedkar (Chairman)
  2. N. Gopalswami Ayyangar
  3. Alladi Krishna Swami Ayyar
  4. K.M. Munshi
  5. Syed Mohammed Saadullah
  6. B.L. Mittar (replaced by N. Madhav Rao due to ill health)
  7. D.P. Khaitan (died in 1948 and was replaced by T.T. Krishnamachari)

COMMITTEES OF CONSTITUENT ASSEMBLY

Committee	Chairman
Drafting Committee	B.R. Ambedkar
Union Constitution Committee	J.L. Nehru
Committee for State Negotiation	Rajendra Prasad
Provincial Constitution.Committee	Sardar Patel
Union Powers Committee	J.L. Nehru
Committee on Fundamental Rights & Minorities	Sardar Patel
The Steering Committee	K.M. Munshi
Rules of Procedure Committee	Rajendra Prasad

FEATURES OF THE CONSTITUTION OF INDIA

1. Three-tier Government
2. Lengthiest Written Constitution
3. Federal System with Unitary Bias
4. Parliamentary Form of Government
5. Synthesis of Parliamentary Sovereignty and Judicial Supremacy
6. Integrated and independent Judiciary
7. Fundamental Rights & Fundamental Duties
8. Directive Principles of State Policy
9. Universal Adult Franchise & Single Citizenship
10. Emergency Provisions
11. Drawn From Various Sources
12. Blend of Rigidity and Flexibility

FEATURES OF INDIAN CONSTITUTION & THEIR SOURCES

Sl.	Feature	Source
1.	Independence of Judiciary	USA
2.	President as the Executive Head & Supreme Commander of Armed Forces	USA
3.	The Vice-President as the ex-officio Chairman of the Council of States	USA
4.	Fundamental Rights	USA
5.	Preamble	USA
6.	Removal of Supreme Court and High Court Judges	USA
7.	Law making procedures	UK
8.	Rule of Law	UK
9.	System of Single Citizenship	UK
10.	Parliamentary System with Ministerial Responsibility	UK
11.	Federation with a strong Centre	Canada
12.	Distribution of powers between the Union and the States and placing residuary powers with the Centre	Canada
13.	Directive Principles of State Policy	Ireland
14.	Method of Election of the President	Ireland
15.	Nomination of members of the Rajya Sabha by the President	Ireland
16.	Emergency and its effect on Fundamental Rights	Germany
17.	The Concurrent List	Australia
18.	Provision regarding Trade, Commerce and Intercourse with the Territory	Australia
19.	Constitution Amendments	South Africa
20.	Fundamental Duties	Japan
21.	Republic	France

SCHEDULES OF THE CONSTITUTION

Schedule	Deals with
First	Name and territorial extent (States and Union Territories)
Second	Emoluments, allowances, privileges of President, Governors, Speakers, etc.
Third	Forms of Oaths or Affirmations
Fourth	Allocation of seats to various States & UTs in the Rajya Sabha (Council of States).
Fifth	Provision as to administration and control of scheduled areas and scheduled tribes
Sixth	Provision as to administration of tribal areas in the State of Assam, Meghalaya, Tripura and Mizoram
Seventh	Division of power between the Union and the States (Union List, State List & Concurrent List)
Eighth	Languages (originally 14 but presently 22) recognized by the Constitution, namely Assamese, Bengali, Dogri, Gujarati, Hindi, Kannada, Kashmiri, Konkani, Maithili, Malayalam, Manipuri, Marathi, Nepali, Oriya, Punjabi, Sanskrit, Santhali, Sindhi, Tamil, Telugu and Urdu. Sindhi was added by the 21st Constitution Amendment Act, 1967 while Konkani, Manipuri and Nepali were added by the 71st Constitution Amendment Act, 1992. Bodo, Dogri, Maithili and Santhali were added by the 92nd Constitution Amendment Act, 2003.

Schedule	Deals with
Ninth	Acts and regulations (this schedule was added by the 1st Constitution Amendment Act, 1951)
Tenth	Disqualification of the members of Parliament and State Legislatures on the ground of defection. This schedule was added by the 52nd Constitution Amendment Act, also known as Anti Defection Act (1985).
Eleventh	Powers, authority and responsibilities of Panchayats. It has 29 subjects. This schedule was added by the 73rd Amendment Act, 1992.
Twelfth	Powers, authority and responsibilities of municipalities. It has 18 subjects. This schedule was added by the 74th Amendment Act, 1992.

PARTS OF THE INDIAN CONSTITUTION

Part	Deals with	Articles
I	The Union and its Territory	1 to 4
II	Citizenship	5 to 11
III	Fundamental Rights	12 to 35
IV	Directive Principles of the State Policy	36 to 51
IV-A	Fundamental Duties (inserted by 42nd Constitution Amendment Act, 1976)	51-A
V	The Union Government	52 to 151
VI	The State Governments	152 to 237
VIII	The Union Territories	239 to 242
IX	The Panchayats (inserted by 73rd Constitution Amendment Act, 1992)	243 to 243-O
IX-A	The Municipalities (inserted by 74th Constitution Amendment Act, 1992)	243-P to 243-ZG
X	The Scheduled and Tribal Areas	244 to 244-A
XI	Relations between the Union and the States	245 to 263
XII	Finance, Property, Contracts and Suits	264 to 300-A
XIII	Trade, Commerce and Intercourse within the Territory of India	301 to 307
XIV	Services under the Union and the States	308 to 323
XIV-A	Tribunals (inserted by 42nd Constitution Amendment Act, 1976)	323-A to 323-B
XV	Elections	324 to 329-A
XVI	Special provisions to SCs, STs, OBCs and Anglo-Indians	330 to 342
XVII	Official Language	343 to 351
XVIII	Emergency Provisions	352 to 360
XIX	Miscellaneous	361 to 367
XX	Amendment of the Constitution	368
XXI	Temporary, Transitional and Special provisions	369 to 392
XXII	Short title, Commencement, Authoritative text in Hindi and Repeals	393 to 395

FUNDAMENTAL RIGHTS

- **Right To Equality**

  Article 14 • Equality before law and equal protection of law.

  Article 15 • Prohibition of discrimination on grounds only of religion, race, caste, sex or place of birth.

  Article 16 • Equality of opportunity in matters of public empolyment.

  Article 17 • End of untouchability.

  Article 18 • Abolition of titles. Military and academic distinctions are, however, exempted.

- **Right To Freedom**

  Article 19 • It guarantees the citizens of India the following six fundamental freedoms:

  (*a*) Freedom of speech and Expression.

  (*b*) Freedom of Assembly

  (*c*) Freedom to form Associations.

  (*d*) Freedom of Movement.

  (*e*) Freedom of Residence and Settlement.

  (*f*) Freedom of Profession, Occupation, Trade or Business.

  Article 20 • Protection in respect of conviction for offences.

  Article 21 • Protection of life and personal liberty.

  Article 22 • Protection against arrest and detention in certain cases.

- **Right Against Exploitation**

  Article 23 • Traffic in human beings prohibited.

  Article 24 • No child below the age of 14 can be employed.

- **Right To Freedom of Religion**

  Article 25 • Freedom of conscience and free profession, practice and propagation of religion.

  Article 26 • Freedom to manage religious affairs.

  Article 27 • Prohibits taxes on religious grounds.

  Article 28 • Freedom as to attendance at religious ceremonies in certain educational institutions

- **Cultural and Education Rights**

  Article 29 • Protection of interests of minorities.

  Article 30 • Right of minorities to establish and administer educational institutions.

  Article 31 • Omitted by the 44th Amendment Act.

- **Right To Constitutional Remedies**

  Article 32 • The right to move the Supreme Court in case of their violation (called *Soul and heart of the Constitution* by BR Ambedkar)

> **Note :** To enforce the Fundamental Rights, the Supreme Court is empowered under Article 32 to issue writs of various forms.

FORMS OF WRITS

Habeas Corpus • Literally means 'to have the body'. Implies that a person imprisoned or detained by the law can enquire under what authority he has been imprisoned or detained.

Mandamus
- Literally means a 'command' issued by the court commanding a person or a public authority to do or forbear to do something in the nature of public duty.

Quo Warranto
- An order issued by the court to prevent a person from holding office to which he is not entitled & to oust him from that office.

Certlorarl
- It is a writ, which orders the removal of a suit from an inferior court to a superior court (for speedy justice).

Prohibition
- By a higher court to stop proceedings in a lower court on the ground of over-stepping of jurisdiction or isolation of the rules of natural justice.

THE NEW STATES CREATED AFTER 1950

Andhra Pradesh
- Created by the State of Andhra Pradesh Act, 1953 by carving out some areas from the State of Chennai.

Gujarat and Maharashtra
- The State of Mumbai was divided into two States, *i.e.*, Maharashtra and Gujarat by the Mumbai (Reorganisation) Act, 1960.

Kerala

Created by the State Reorganisation Act, 1956. It comprised Travancor and Cochin areas.

Karnataka
- Created from the Princely State of Mysuru by the State Reorganisation Act,1956. It was renamed Karnataka in 1973.

Nagaland
- It was carved out from the State of Asom by the State of Nagaland Act, 1962.

Haryana
- It was carved out from the State of Punjab by the Punjab Reorganisation Act, 1966.

Himachal Pradesh
- The Union Territory of Himachal Pradesh was elevated to the status of State by the State of Himachal Pradesh Act, 1970.

Meghalaya
- First carved out as a sub-State within the State of Asom by 23rd Constitutional Amendment Act, 1969. Later, in 1971, it received the status of a full-fledged State by the North-Eastern Areas (Reorganisation) Act, 1971.

Manipur and Tripura
- Both these States were elevated from the status of Union Territories by the North-Eastern Areas (Reorganisation) Act, 1971.

Sikkim
- Sikkim was first given the Status of Associate State by the 35th Constitutional Amendment Act, 1974. It got the Status of a full State in 1975 by the 36th Amendment Act, 1975.

Mizoram
- It was elevated to the status of a full State by the State of Mizoram Act, 1986.

Arunachal Pradesh
- It received the status of a full State by the State of Arunachal Pradesh Act, 1986.

Goa
- Goa was separated from the Union Territory of Goa, Daman and Diu and was made a full-fledged State by the Goa, Daman and Diu Reorganisation Act, 1987. But Daman and Diu remained as Union Territory.

Chhattisgarh
- Formed by the Constitutional Amendment Act, 2000 by dividing Madhya Pradesh on November 1, 2000.

Uttarakhand • Formed by the Constitutional Amendment Act, 2000 by dividing Uttar Pradesh on November 9, 2000.

Jharkhand • Formed by the Constitutional Amendment Act, 2000 by dividing Bihar on November 15, 2000.

Telangana • Formed by Andhra Pradesh reorganisation act 2014.

IMPORTANT CONSTITUTIONAL AMENDMENT ACTS

Number of Constitutional Amendment Act	Year	Amended Subjects
First	1951	• Right to equality, Right to liberty and Right to property were restricted in public interest. • The Land Reform Acts were put into Ninth Schedule to make them out of jurisdiction of the Courts. • The sessions of legislatures, appointment of judges and provision of seats were also affected.
Seventh	1956	• State reorganisation in 14 States and 6 Union Territories. Reallocation of seats in the House of the People, the Council of States and the State legislatures. • Provision for the appointment of acting and additional judges and jurisdiction of High Courts. • Provisions for Union Territories. • Special provisions for the States of Andhra Pradesh, Punjab and Bombay.
Fifteenth	1963	• The retirement age of the Judges of the High Courts was raised to 62 years from 60 years. • Provision for the re-employment of the retired judge of the High Courts. • Extension to the jurisdiction of the High Courts.
Twentieth	1966	Provisions regarding appointment to District Judges.
Twenty seventh	1971	Reorganisation of North-Eastern States.
Forty-second	1976	• The words 'Secular', 'Socialist' and 'Integrity' added in the Preamble, • The validity of the Constitutional Amendment can not be questioned any Court-368 (4) • Extension of the Directive Principles of State Policy. • Primacy given to the Directive Principles of State Policy over the Fundamental Rights. • The Fundamental Duties added. • Restriction on the Fundamental Rights widened. • The power of Judicial Review of the Courts was restricted. • The duration of the House of the People and the Legislative Assemblies of the State extended to 6 years. • Provisions were made for the participation of the workers in-the management of industries.

Number of Constitutional Amendment Act	Year	Amended Subjects
		• Provisions for the protection of environment, forests and wildlife. • Provisions for the protection of the children and the youth against exploitation. • No quorum shall be required for conducting the meeting of the House of the People and the Legislative Assemblies of the States. • The Right of the Supreme Court to examine the validity of the laws of the State under Art. 32A abolished. • The Jury System was given importance in the functioning of the Courts. • The President shall be bound by the advice of the Council of Ministers. • The Central Government was given the power to send Central Forces in any State or part of State to control the law and order in that State and the control of such forces shall rest with the Central Government. • Emergency Provisions : (*a*) National Emergency may be proclaimed in a part of the Territory of India; (*b*) The one time duration of the President rule in a State under the Art. 356 was extended from 6 months to one year. • Some subjects – protection of the forest and the wildlife, education, weight and measures, population control and judicial administration shifted to the Concurrent List. • Provisions for the establishment of the administrative tribunals for public servants.
Fourty-fourth	1978	• The Fundamental Right to Property was abolished. • The term of the Lok Sabha and the Legislative Assemblies of the States reduced to 5 years. • The disputes relating to the qualifications of the members of the Parliament and the State Legislature shall be decided by the President and the Governors, respectively. • The provisions regarding quorum in the legislatures was changed to as these were before 42nd Amendment. • It was provided that disputes relating to the election of the President and the Vice-President shall be decided by the Supreme Court and that of the election of the member of the Parliament and the State legislature shall be decided by the High Courts. • The national emergency shall not be proclaimed except on the written recommendation of the cabinet.
Sixty-first	1988	The minimum age limit prescribed to get the Voting Right was reduced to 18 years from 21 years.

Number of Constitutional Amendment Act	Year	Amended Subjects
Sixty-fifth	1990	The National Commission for the Scheduled Castes and the Scheduled Tribes was given a Constitutional Status.
Sixty-ninth	1991	The Union Territory of Delhi was named as the National Capital Territory of Delhi. It also provided for a 70-member State Assembly for Delhi.
Seventy-third	1992	Provisions relating to the Constitution, elections, finance and functions of the Panchayati Raj bodies.
Seventy-fourth	1992	Provisions relating to the Constitution, election, finance and functions of the municipalities.
Seventy-fifth	1994	Provisions for the establishment of a Special Administrative Tribunal for the speedy disposal of the disputes between the householders and the tenants.
Eighty-third	2000	It provides that no reservation in Panchayats need to be made in favour of the Scheduled Castes in Arunachal Pradesh wholly inhabited by the tribal population.
Eighty-fourth	2001	Creation of the new States of Chhattisgarh, Uttaranchal and Jharkhand.
Eighty-fifth	2001	It provided for consequential seniority in the case of promotion by virtue of rule of reservation for the Government Servants belonging to the SCs & STs with retrospective effect from June 1995.
Eighty-sixth	2002	• It made elementary education a fundamental right. • It changed the subject matter of Art. 45 in Directive Principles. • It added a new Fundamental Duty under Art. 51 A.
Eighty-seventh	2003	It provided for the readjustment and rationalization territorial constituencies in the States on the basis of the population figures of 2001 Census and not 1991 Census.
Eighty-eighth	2003	It made a provision for service tax by inserting Art. 268 A. Taxes on services are levied by the Centre but there proceeds are collected as well as appropriated by both the Centre and the States in accordance with the principles formulated by the Parliament.
Eighty-ninth	2003	It bifurcated National Commission for SCs and STs into two separate bodies, namely National Commission for SCs (Art. 338) and National Commission for STs (Art. 338 A)
Nineieth	2003	It provided for maintaining the erstwhile representation of the STs and non STs in the Assam Legislative Assembly from the Bodoland Territorial Areas District [Art. 332(6)].
Ninety-first	2003	• The total number of ministers including the Prime Minister in the central Council of Ministers shall not exceed 15% of the total strength of the Lok Sabha [Art. 75(1 A)].

Number of Constitutional Amendment Act	Year	Amended Subjects
		• A member of either House of Parliament belonging to any political party who is disqualified on the ground of defection shall also be disqualified to be appointed as a minister. [Art. 75 (1B)]. • The total number of ministers including the Chief Ministers in the Council of the Ministers in a State shall not exceed 15% of the total strength of the Legislative Assembly of that State. But the number of ministers including the Chief Minister in a State shall not be less than 12 [Art. 164 (1 A)]. • The provision of the tenth Schedule (Anti-Defection Law) pertaining to exemption from disqualification in case of split by 1/3rd members of the legislature party has been deleted. It means that the defectors have no more protection on grounds of splits.
Ninety-second	2003	It included four more languages in the eighth Schedule, viz. Bodo, Dogri (Dongri), Mathilli (Maithili) and Santhali. With this, the total number of constitutionally recognised languages increased to 22.
Ninety-third	2005	It impowered the State to make special provisions for the socially and educationally backward classes or the SCs or STs in educational institutions including private educational institution (whether aided or unaided by the State), except the minority educational institutions [clause (5) in Art. 15].
Ninety-fourth	2006	It freed Bihar from the obligation of having a tribal welfare minister and extended the same provision to Jharkhand and Chhattisgarh [Art. 164(1)].
Ninety-fifth	2010	To extend the reservation of seats for SCs and STs in the Lok Sabha and states assemblies from Sixty years to Seventy years
Ninety-sixth	2011	Substituted "Odia" for "Oriya"
Ninety-seventh	2012	Added the words "or co-operative societies" after the word "or unions" in Article 19(l)(c) and insertion of article 43B i.e., Promotion of Co-operative Societies and added Part-IXB i.e., The Co-operative Societies. The amendment objective is to encourage economic activities of cooperatives which in turn help progress of rural India. It is expected to not only ensure autonomous and democratic functioning of cooperatives, but also the accountability of the management to the members and other stakeholders.[101]

Ninety-eighth	2013	To empower the Governor of Karnataka to take steps to develop the Hyderabad-Karnataka Region.[102]
Ninety-ninth	2015	The amendment provides for the formation of a National Judicial Appointments Commission. 16 State assemblies out of 29 States including Goa, Rajasthan, Tripura, Gujarat and Telangana ratified the Central Legislation, enabling the President of India to give assent to the bill.[105] The amendment was struck down by the Supreme Court on 16 October 2015.
Hundredth	2015	Exchange of certain enclave territories with Bangladesh and conferment of citizenship rights to residents of enclaves consequent to signing of Land Boundary Agreement (LBA) Treaty between India and Bangladesh
Hundred and one	2017	Goods and Services Tax Act

PRESIDENT

Qualifications

- Must be a citizen of India.
- Completed 35 yrs in age.
- Eligible to be a member of Lok Sabha,
- Must not hold any Government post. Exceptions:
  (*i*) President and Vice- President
  (*ii*) Governor of any State
  (*iii*) Minister of Union or State.

Election

- Indirectly elected through 'Electoral Collage' consisting of Elected members of both the Houses of Parliament & Elected members of the Legislative Assemblies of the States. (No nominated members).
- Security deposit -15.000/-
- Supreme Court inquires all disputes regarding President's election.
- Takes OATH in presence of Chief Justice of India, or in his absence, senior-most judge of Supreme Court.

Term & Emoluments

- 5 year term.
- Article 57 says that there is no upper limit on the no. of times a person can become President.
- Can give resignation to Vice-president before full-term.
- Present Salary ₹5,00,000/month (including allowances & emoluments).

Impeachment

- Quasi-judicial procedure.
- Can be impeached only on the ground of violation of Constitution
- The impeachment procedure can be initiated in either House of the Parliament.

Vacancy

- In case the office falls vacant dua to death, resignation or removal, the Vice-President acts as President. If he is not available then Chief Justice, if not then senior-most judge of Supreme Court shall act as the President of India.
- The election is to be held within 6 months of the vacancy.

Powers

- Appoints PM, ministers, Chief Justice & judges of Supreme Court & High Courts, Chairman & members of UPSC, Comptroller and Auditor General, Attorney General, Chief Election Commissioner and other members of Election Commission, Governors, Members of Finance Commission. Ambassadors, etc.
- Can summon & prorogue the sessions of the 2 houses & can dissolve Lok Sabha.
- Appoints Finance Commission (after every 5 yrs) that recommends distribution of taxes between Union & State govts.
- Appoints the Chief Justice and the judges of the Supreme Court and High Courts.
- The President can promulgate 3 types of Emergencies :
  (*i*) National Emergency (Article 352)
  (*ii*) State Emergency (President's Rule) (Article 356)
  (*iii*) Financial Emergency (Article 360)
- He is the Supreme Commander of the Defence Forces of India.
- President appoints Chiefs of Army, Navy & Air Force.
- Declares wars & concludes peace subject to the approval of the Parliament.

• PRESIDENTS OF INDIA

Name	Tenure	
	From	To
Dr. Rajendra Prasad	26.01.1950	13.05.1962
Dr. S. Radhakrishnan	13.05.1962	13 05.1967
Dr. Zakir Hussain	13.05.1967	03.05.1969
V.V. Giri (Vice-President)#	03.05.1969	20.07.1969
Justice M. Hidayatullah *#	20.07.1969	24.08.1969

Name	Tenure	
	From	To
V.V. Giri	24.08.1969	24.08.1974
F. Ali Ahmed	24.08.1974	11.02 1977
B.D. Jatti#	11.02.1977	25.07.1977
N. Sanjiva Reddy	25.07.1977	25.07 1982
Gyani Jail Singh	25.07.1982	25.07.1987
R. Venkataraman	25.07.1987	25.07.1992
Dr. S.D. Sharma	25.07.1992	25.07.1997
K.R. Narayanan	25.07.1997	25.07.2002
Dr. A.P. J. Abdul Kalam	25.07.2002	24.07.2007
Mrs. Pratibha Patil	25.07.2007	25.07.2012
Pranab Mukherjee	25.07.2012	25.07.2017
Ram Nath Kovind	25.07.2017	Till date
# **Acting; * First Chief-Justice to be appointed President.**		

VICE-PRESIDENT

Election

- Elected by both the houses (Electoral College) in accordance with the system of proportional representation by means of single transferable vote and the vote being secret. Nominated members also participate in his election.
- The Supreme Court has the final and exclusive jurisdiction for resolving disputes and doubts **relating** to the **election of the Vice-President.**

Criteria

- Citizen of India.
- More than 36 years of age.
- Passess the qualification for membership of Rajya Sabha.
- Not hold any office of profit under union, state or local authority. However, for this purpose, the President, Vice-President, Governor of a State and Minister of the Union or a State, are not held to be holding an office of profit.

Other Points

- Holds office for 5 yrs. Can be re-elected.
- Term can be cut short if he resigns or by a resolution of the Rajya Sabha passed by a majority of all the members of the Rajya Sabha and agreed to by the Lok Sabha.
- He is the ex-officio Chairman of Rajya Sabha. Since he is not a member of Rajya Sabha, he has no right to vote.
- Being the Vice-President of India, he is not entitled for any salary, but he is entitled to the salary and allowances payable to the Chairman of the Rajya Sabha.
- All bills, resolution, motion can be taken in Rajya Sabha after his consent.
- Can discharge the function of President if the post falls vacant. (For maximum 6 months).
- When he discharges the functions of the President, the Vice-President shall not perform the duties of the office of the Chairman of Rajya Sabha and shall not be entitled to receive the salary of the Chairman. During this period, he is entitled for the salary and privileges of the President of india.
- Present salary is ₹ 1,25,000/- per month.

• VICE-PRESIDENTS OF INDIA

Name	Tenure	
	From	To
Dr. Sarvepalli Radhakrishnan	1952	1962
Dr. Zakir Hussain	1962	1967
V.V. Giri	1967	1969
Bal Swaroop Pathak	1969	1974
Dr. M. Jatti	1974	1979
Justice Mohd. Hidayatullah	1979	1984
S. Venkataraman	1984	1987
Dr. Shankar Dayal Sharma	1987	1992
K.R. Narayanan	1992	1997
Krishan Kant	1997	2002
Bhairon Singh Shekhawat	2002	2007
Hamid Ansari	2007	2017
Venkaiah Naidu	2017	Till date

PRIME MINISTER

Powers

- Real executive authority.
- He is the ex-officio Chairman of the Planning Commission, National Development Council, National Integration Council and Inter-state Council.
- The President convenes and prorogues all sessions of Parliament in consultation with him.
- Can recommend the dissolution of Lok Sabha before expiry.
- Appoints the Council of ministers.
- Allocates portfolios. Can ask a minister to resign & can get him dismissed by President.
- Assists the President in appointment of all high officials.
- Can recommend to the President to declare emergency on grounds of war, external aggression or armed rebellion.
- Advises President about President's Rule in the State or emergency due to financial instability.
- Leader of the House.

• PRIME MINISTERS OF INDIA

Name	Tenure	
	From	To
Jawahar Lal Nehru	15.08.1947	27.05.1964
Gulzari Lai Nanda*	27.05.1964	09.06.1964
Lal Bahadur Shastri	09.06.1964	11.01.1966
Gulzari Lal Nanda*	11.01.1966	24.01.1966
Indira Gandhi	24.01.1966	24.03.1977
Morarji Desai	24.03.1977	28.07.1979

Name	Tenure	
	From	To
Charan Singh	28.07.1979	14.01.1980
Indira Gandhi	14.01.1980	31.10.1984
Rajiv Gandhi	31.10.1984	01.12.1989
V.P. Singh	01.12.1989	10.11.1990
Chandra Shekhar	10.11.1990	21.06.1991
P.V. Narsimha Rao	21.06.1991	16.05.1996
Atal Bihari Vajpayee	16.05.1996	01.06.1996
H.D. Deve Gowda	01.06.1996	21.04.1997
I.K. Gujral	21.04.1997	19.03.1998
Atal Bihari Vajpayee	19.03.1998	13.10.1999
Atal Bihari Vajpayee	13.10.1999	22.05.2004
Dr. Manmohan Singh	22.05.2004	26.05.2014
Narendra Modi	26.05.2014	Till date

PARLIAMENT OF INDIA

Lok Sabha

- Maximum strength - 550 + 2 nominated members.
  [530 - States / 20 - Union Territories]
- Present strength of Lok Sabha - 545.
- The Eighty Fourth Amendment, 2001, extended freeze on Lok Sabha and State Assembly seats till 2026.
- The normal tenure of the Lok Sabha is five years, but it may be dissolved earlier by the President. The life of the Lok Sabha can be extended by the Parliament beyond the five year term, when a proclamation of emergency under Article 352 is in force.

  But the Parliament cannot extend the normal life of the Lok Sabha for more than one year at a time (no limit on the number of times in the Constitution).
- The candidate must be :
  (*a*) Citizen of India.
  (*b*) Atleast 25 yrs of age.
  (*c*) Mustn't hold any office of profit.
  (*d*) No unsound mind / insolvent.
  (*e*) Has registered as voter in any Parliamentary constituency.
- Oath of MPs is conducted by the Speaker. Can resign, by writing to Speaker.
- Presiding officer is Speaker (In his absence Deputy Speaker). The members among themselves elect him.
- The Speaker continues in office even after the dissolution of the Lok Sabha till a newly elected Lok Sabha meets.
- Usually the Speaker, after his election cuts-off all connection with his party & acts in an impartial manner. He does not vote in the first instance, but exercises his casting vote only to remove a deadlock.

- Charges his salary from Consolidated Fund of India.
- Speaker sends his resignation to deputy Speaker.
- The majority of the total membership can remove Speaker after giving a 14 days notice. (During this time, he doesn't preside over the meetings). After his removal, continues in office till his successor takes charge.

Rajya Sabha

- Maximum Strength - 250
- Out of these, President nominates 12 amongst persons having special knowledge or practical experience in the fields of literature, science, art and social service.
- Presently, the Parliament, by law, has provided for 233 seats for the States and the Union Territories. The total membership of Rajya Sabha is thus 245.
- All the States and the Union Territories of Delhi and Puducherry are represented in the Rajya Sabha.
- Representatives of the State are elected by members of State legislative assemblies on the basis of proportional representation through a single transferable vote. [States are represented on the basis of their population].
- There are no seats reserved for Scheduled Castes and Scheduled Tribes in Rajya Sabha.
- The candidate must be :

  (*a*) Citizen of India.

  (*b*) 30 yrs of age.

  (*c*) Be a parliamentary elector in the State in which he is seeking election.

  (*d*) Others as prescribed by parliament from time-to-time.
- The Rajya Sabha MPs are elected for a term of 6 years, as 1/3rd members retire every 2 years.
- Vice-President is the ex-officio Chairman of Rajya Sabha. He presides over the proceedings of the Rajya Sabha as long as he does not act as the President of India during a vacancy in the office of the President of India.
- Also a deputy Chairman is elected from its members.
- In Rajya Sabha any bill can originate, apart from money bill (including budget).

- **REPRESENTATION OF STATES AND AND UNION TERRITORIES**

State/UTs	Lok Sabha	Rajya Sabha
Andhra Pradesh	25	18
Arunachal Pradesh	2	1
Assam	14	7
Bihar	40	16
Chhattisgarh	11	
Goa	2	1
Gujarat	26	
Haryana	10	

State/UTs	Lok Sabha	Rajya Sabha
Himachal Pradesh	4	3
Jammu & Kashmir	6	4
Jharkhand	14	
Karnataka	28	12
Kerala	20	9
Madhya Pradesh	29	11
Maharashtra	48	19
Manipur	2	1
Meghalaya	2	1
Mizoram	1	1
Nagaland	1	1
Odisha	21	10
Punjab	13	7
Rajasthan	25	10
Sikkim	1	1
Tamil Nadu	39	18
Telangana	17	
Tripura	2	1
Uttar Pradesh	80	31
Uttarakhand	5	3
West Bengal	42	16
Union Territory		
Andaman & Nicobar	1	—
Chandigarh	1	—
Dadra & Nagar Haveli	1	—
Daman & Diu	1	—
Delhi	7	3
Lakshadweep	1	—
Puducherry	1	1

SUPREME COURT OF INDIA

Status

- Stands at the apex of the judicial system of India.
- Consists of Chief Justice & 30 other judges.

Appointment

- The senior-most judge of the Supreme Court is appointed as the chief Justice of India. Other judges are appointed by the President after consultation with such judges of the Supreme Court and of the High Courts as the President may deem necessary.

Qualification

- Citizen of India.
- Have been a judge of High Court for 5 yrs or
  (*i*) An advocate of High Court for 10 years minimum or
  (*ii*) In President's view, a distinguished jurist of the country.

Term & Salary

- The Chief Justice & other judges hold office till 65 yrs of age.
- Can give resignation to President.
- Can be removed by the Parliament.
- After retirement, a judge of Supreme Court cannot plead or act before any authority.
- **Salary :**
  Chief Justice — ₹ 2.8 lakhs per month
  Other Judges of SC — ₹ 2.5 lakhs per month

Removal of Judges

- A motion seeking the removal of the judge can be preferred before either House of the Parliament.
- The resolution should be supported by a majority of total membership of both the houses & by 2/3 majority of the members present & voting.

Jurisdiction of the Supreme Court

- **Original Jurisdiction :** The Supreme Court settles all disputes between Centre-State, State - State, etc.
- **Writ Jurisdiction :** Every individual has the right to move the Supreme Court directly by appropriate proceedings for the enforcement of his Fundamental Rights.
- **Advisory Jurisdiction :** If the President seeks the advice of Supreme Court, it is duty bound to give its opinion. (Its opinion isn't a binding on President).
- **Revisory Jurisdiction :** The Supreme Court under *Article 137* is empowered to review any judgement or order made by it with a view to removing any mistake or error that might have crept in the judgement or order.
- It is a court of record as its decisions are of evidentiary value & cannot be questioned in any court.
- The Supreme Court also enjoys the power of judicial review as it can ensure that the laws passed by legislature and orders issued by the executive do not contravene any provision of the Constitution.
- The Supreme Court decides disputes regarding the election of the President and the Vice President.
- The Supreme Court recommends the removal of members to UPSC to the President.

THE GOVERNOR

Qualifications

- Citizen of India
- Completed 35 years of age.
- Shouldn't be a member of either House of Parliament or the State Legislature.
- Must possess the qualification for membership of State Legislature.
- Mustn't hold any office of profit.

Status

- Nominal executive head in States.
- Normally each State has its own Governor, but under the Seventh Amendment Act 1956, the same person can be appointed as Governor of one or more States or Lt. Governor of the Union Territory.
- Appointed by the President on the recommendations of Union Council of Ministers.
- His usual term of office is 5 years but he holds office during the pleasure of the President. He can be asked to continue for more time until his successor takes the charge.
- Can give his resignation or can be removed earlier by the President. The Legislature of a State or a High Court has no role in the removal of a Governor.
- Salary from the Consolidated Fund of the State (₹ 1,00,000 per month) and is not subject to the vote of the State Legislature. When the same person is appointed as the Governor of two or more States, the emoluments and allowances payable to him shall be allocated among the States in such proportion as determined by the President of India.
- His oath is administered by the Chief Justice of the concerned State High Court and in his absence, the senior-most judge of that Court.

Powers

- Appoints Chief Minister, Council of Ministers. Chairman & members of State Public Service Commission, Advocate General of the State and Election Commissioner of the State.
- Summons, Prorogues & dissolves the State Legislature.
- President consults to Governor while appointing Chief Justice and other judges ot High Court. Appoints judges of courts below the High Court.
- Reports to the President if the State Government is not running constitutionally and recommends the President's Rule (Article 356). When the Presidents Rule is in progress, he becomes the 'Agent of the Union Government in the State'. He takes over the resigns of administration directly into his own hands and runs the State with the aid of the Civil Servants.

CHIEF MINISTER

Status

- Real executive head of the Govt. at the State level.
- The position of Chief Minister at the State level is analogous to the position of the Prime Minister at the Centre.
- Appointed by Governor. Other Ministers are appointed by the Governor on the advice of the Chief Minister.
- If Chief minister resigns, entire ministry resigns.
- Generally, the leader of the majority party is appointed.
- A person who is not a member of State Legislature can be appointed, but he has to get himself elected within 6 months otherwise he is removed.

STATE LEGISLATURE

Status	• Can be : 1. UNICAMERAL [One House] 2. BICAMERAL [Two House] • Bicameral Status : 6 States : (*i*) Bihar-75 (*ii*) J&K-36 (*iii*) Karnataka - 75 (*iv*) Maharashtra - 78. (*v*) UP - 104 (*vi*) Andhra Pradesh - 90 [2 other States were Andhra Pradesh & Tamil Nadu]. • Legislative Council can be created or abolished on the recommendation of Legislative Assembly.

LEGISLATIVE COUNCIL (Vidhan Parishad)

Status	• Also known as Upper House. Like Rajya Sabha, it is also a Permanent House (sort of) and cannot be dissolved.
Strength	• The total strength cannot exceed 1/3rd of the strength of Legislative Assembly, subject to a minimum of 40 members. The strength varies as per the population of State.
Creation and Abolition	• If the Legislative Assembly passes a resolution for abolishing or creating of the Legislative Council by a majority of the total membership of the assembly and by a majority of not less than two-third of the members present and voting, the Parliament may approve the resolution by a simple majority. • A resolution passed by the Legislative Assembly for the creation or abolition of its Council is not binding on the Parliament. The Parliament may or may not approve such a situation.
Tenure	• 6 yrs term with 1/3rd members retiring every two years.
Qualification	• Same as that of Lok Sabha, except the age which is 30 yrs.
Election	• One-third of the members are elected by local bodies, one - third by Legislative Assembly, one-twelfth by university graduates of atleast 3 yrs standing, similar proportion by teachers (not less than secondary school) of atleast 3 yrs standing & one-sixth nominated by the Governor from among those persons who distinguish themselves in literature, science or social service.
Chairman	• The council elects a Chairman & a Vice-chairman among its members.

LEGISLATIVE ASSEMBLY (Vidhan Sabha)

Status
- Also known as Lower House, just like the Lok Sabha.

Strength
- Consists of not more than 525 members & not less than 60 members. The strength varies according to the population of the State concerned. However, the Legislative Assembly of Sikkim has only 32 members.
- Consists of directly elected representatives.
- Has a term of 5 yrs but can be dissolved by the Governor earlier. Term can be extended by one year during national emergency.

Qualification
- Same as that of Lok Sabha or Legislative Council except that the minimum age is 25 yrs.
- The Council of Ministers is collectively responsible to the Assembly. The assembly chooses its own Speaker & Deputy Speaker who can be removed by Council of Ministers. The Chief Minister is the leader of the House.

Powers of State Legislature
- Can legislate on subjects contained in the State List as well as Concurrent List.
- Exercise control over state expenses.
- Exercise control over State Council of Ministers (can even remove it by passing the no-confidence motion).
- Participates in the election of the President.
- Has a share in the Amendment of Constitution as some provisions can be amended after ratification by the legislatures of half of the States.

• STRENGTH OF STATE LEGISLATURES

States/UTs	Legislative Assembly	Legislative Council
Andhra Pradesh	294	90
Arunachal Pradesh	40	Nil
Assam	126	Nil
Delhi	70	Nil
Bihar	243	75
Maharashtra	288	78
Manipur	60	Nil
Meghalaya	60	Nil
Mizoram	40	Nil
Nagaland	60	Nil
Jharkhand	81	Nil

States/UTs	Legislative Assembly	Legislative Council
Jharkhand	81	Nil
Goa	40	Nil
Gujarat	182	Nil
Haryana	90	Nil
Himachal Pradesh	68	Nil
Jammu & Kashmir	76	36
Karnataka	224	75
Kerala	140	Nil
Madhya Pradesh	230	Nil
Chhattisgarh	90	Nil
Odisha	147	Nil
Puducherry	30	Nil
Punjab	117	Nil
Rajasthan	200	Nil
Sikkim	32	Nil
Tamil Nadu	234	Nil
Tripura	60	Nil
Uttar Pradesh	403	104
Uttarakhand	70	Nil
West Bengal	294	Nil

HIGH COURT

Status

- Each State has a High Court; it is the highest judicial organ of the State.
- However, there can be a common High Court like Punjab, Haryana & Union Territory of Chandigarh. Presently there are 21 High Courts in India.
- Consists of Chief Justice & other such judges as appointed by the President.
- The Constitution, unlike in the case of the Supreme Court, does not fix any maximum number of judges for a High Court. (Allahabad High Court has 37 judges while J&K High Court has only 5).
- A judge of a High Court can be transferred to another High Court without his consent by the President. In this, the Chief Justice of India is also consulted. The opinion provided by him shall have primacy and is binding on the President.

Appointment of Judges

- The appointment of Chief Justice is made after consultation with the Chief Justice of Supreme Court & the Governor of the State by the President. In case of appointment of a Judge, the Chief Justice of the High Court concerned is also consulted in addition to Chief Justice of Supreme Court & Governor of the State concerned.

Qualification

- Must be a citizen of India.
- Should have been an advocate of a High Court or of two such Courts in succession for atleast 10 yrs; or should have held judicial office in India for a period of atleast 10 yrs.

Term & Salary

- A judge of High Court continues his office till 62 yrs of age. Term can be cut short due to resignation or removal by the President. The Salary of the Chief Justice is ₹ 90,000 per month, while that of other judges is ₹ 80,000 p.m.

Removal

- The President can remove a judge of High Court only if the Parliament passes the resolution by a 2/3 majority of its members present & voting in each house.
- The conduct of the judges of the High Court cannot be discussed in Parliament, except on a motion for the removal of a judge.

• JURISDICTION AND SEATS OF HIGH COURTS

Name	Estd. in the year	Territorial Jurisdiction	Seat
Allahabad	1866	Uttar Pradesh	Allahabad (Bench at Lucknow)
Andhra Pradesh	1954	Andhra Pradesh	Hyderabad
Mumbai	1862	Maharashtra, Dadra and Nagar Haveli, Goa, Damah and Diu	Mumbai (Bench at Nagpur Panaji and Aurangabad)
Kolkata	1862	West Bengal and Andaman and Nicobar	Kolkata (Circuit Bench at Port Blair)
Delhi	1966	Delhi	Delhi
Guwahati	1948	Asom, Manipur, Meghalaya, Nagaland, Tripura, Mizoram and Arunachal Pradesh	Guwahati (Bench at Kohima and Circuit Benches at Imphal, Agartala & Shillong)
Gujarat	1960	Gujarat	Ahmedabad
Himachal Pradesh	1971	Himachal Pradesh	Shimla
J&K	1957	J&K	Srinagar and Jammu
Karnataka	1884	Karnataka	Bangaluru
Kerala	1956	Kerala and Lakshadweep	Ernakularm
Madhya Pradesh	1956	Madhya Pradesh	Jabalpur (Benches at Gwalior and Indore)

Name	Estd. in the year	Territorial Jurisdiction	Seat
Chennai	1862	Tamil Nadu and Puducherry	Chennai
Odisha	1948	Odisha	Cuttack
Patna	1916	Bihar	Patna
Punjab & Haryana	1966	Punjab,Haryana and Chandigarh	Chandigarh
Rajasthan	1950	Rajasthan	Jodhpur (Bench at Jaipur)
Sikkim	1975	Sikkim	Gangtok
Bilaspur	2000	Chhattisgarh	Bilaspur
Nainital	2000	Uttarakhand	Nainital
Ranchi	2000	Jharkhand	Ranchi

UNION PUBLIC SERVICE COMMISSION [UPSC]

Status

- Composition is determined by the President.
- The members of the UPSC are appointed for a term of 6 yrs, or till they attain 65 years of age.
- Can resign earlier to the President.
- President can remove them by issuing orders. Only the Supreme Court makes such a recommendation on the basis of an inquiry.
- Members of the UPSC are not eligible for employment by the Govt. after retirement.

Functions

- To conduct exams for appointment to services under the Union.
- Advise the President (not obligatory on him) in matters relating to appointments, promotions & transfers from one service to another of civil servants.
- All disciplinary matters affecting a person in the service of Union.
- Matters regarding award of pension and awards in respect to injuries sustained during service under the govt.
- Maintains continuity of administration.

ELECTION COMMISSION (Artice 324)

Status

- The Constitution provides for an independent election commission to ensure free and fair election to the Parliament, the State Legislature and the offices of President and Vice-President.
- Consists of Chief Election Commissioner + 2 Election Commissioners. They all enjoy equal powers.
- The Chief Election Commissioner is appointed by the President and the other Election Commissioners are appointed by the President after consultation with the Chief Election Commissioner. Article 324 also provides for the appointment of Regional Commissioners at the time of General Elections after consultation with the Election Commission.
- Election Commissioners are appointed for a term of 5 yrs.
- They are not eligible for re-appointment. Also, they cannot hold any office of profit after their retirement.
- The term of 5 years can by cut short by resignation or removal by President on recommendation of the Parliament (*Sams as that of Judge of the Supreme Court*).

Functions

- Preparation of electoral rolls & keeping voters list updated.
- Preparation of code of conduct for all political parties.
- Recognition of various political parties & allotment of election symbols.
- Appointment of election officers to look into disputes concerning election arrangements.
- To examine the returns of election expenses filed by the candidate.

■ ■

INDIAN ECONOMY

OUTLINE OF INDIAN ECONOMY

Nature

- **Mixed Economy** Existence of both public and private sectors. This term was coined by **JM Keynes.**
- **Agrarain Economy** Even after six-decades of independence 58% of the work force of India is still agriculturist and its contribution to **GNP** is 17.5% in 2010-11.

Features

(*i*) Slow growth of national and per capital income.

(*ii*) Capital deficiency and low rate of capital formation, hence low rate of investment, low production, etc; poor quality of human capital.

(*iii*) Over-dependence on agriculture along with low productivity in agriculture; heavy population pressure.

(*iv*) Unequal distribution of income and wealth.

(*v*) Mass poverty, chronic inflation and chronic unemployment.

Classification

- According to the **World Development Report** (2012), sub-titled **Gender Equity** and **Development,** India with its per capita income of US $ 1340 is placed in lower middle income countries in 2010.
- Even on PPP (Purchasing Power Parity) basis India with US $ 3560 is placed in middle income countries in 2010.
- India has a share of 17.4% in world population but accounts for only 2.3% of world GNI on exchange rate basis.

Socio-Economic Indicators

- Per capita daily intake calorie is 2496 (in 1999).
- Poverty level more than 37% (Tendulkar Committee).
- With **HDI** value of 0.547, India ranked 134/187, and hence has a medium human development (HDR 2011).
- Inequality in India, in terms of Gini co-efficient of 0.36 is huge.
- Illiteracy more than one-fourth of population.

Issues in Development

(*i*) Low per capita income and low rate of economic growth.

(*ii*) High proportion of people below the poverty line.

(*iii*) Low level of productive efficiency due to inadequate nutrition and malnutrition.

(*iv*) Imbalance between population size, resources and capital.

(*v*) Problem of unemployment.

(*vi*) Instability of output of agriculture and related sectors.

(*vii*) Imbalance between heavy industry and wage goods.

(*viii*) imbalance in distribution and growing inequalities.

Planning in India

Historical Milestones

1. **Planned Economy of India** (1934) M Visvesvaraya
2. **National Planning Committee** (1938) Jawaharlal Nehru
3. **Bombay Plan** (1944)
4. **Gandhian Plan** (1944) SN Agarwal
5. **People's Plan** (1945) MN Roy
6. **Sarvodaya Plan** (1950) JP Narayan
7. **Planning Commission** (1950) was set up under the Chairmanship of Pt Jawaharlal Nehru (Gulzarilal Nanda was the first Deputy Chairman)

- *Economic Planning is mentioned in the Concurrent List of VII Schedule of the Indian Constitution and embodies the objectives of Directive Principles of State Policy.*
- Basic Aim of Economic Planning is to bring rapid economic growth through agriculture, industry, power and all other sectors of the economy.

FIVE YEAR PLANS AT A GLANCE

Plan	Emphasis of Plan	Growth Rate	
		Target	Achieved
First Plan (1951-56) *(Based on Herold-Domar Model)*	1/3rd of total expenditure kept aside for agricultural development.	2.1%	3.6%
Second Plan (1956-61) *(Based on P C Mahalanobis two sector model)*	Its objective was rapid industrialization. Three big industries were established at Bhillai (USSR);Durgapur (UK) and Rourkela (West Germany). Locomotive factory at Chittaranjan and Coach factory at Perambur were established.	4.5%	4.1%
Third Plan (1961-66)	Self-reliant and self-generating economy was the goal; Indian economy entered the take-off stage; continued emphasis on heavy and basic industries. This plan is also called **Gadgil Yojana.**	5.6%	2.8%
Plan Holiday (1966-69) and Three Annual Plans were formulated on account of **Indo-Pak Conflict**, two successive years of drought, devolution of currency by 36% and general rise in prices.			
Fourth Plan (1969-74)	• Growth with stability and progressive achieve-ment of self-reliance. • **Growth with Justice and Garibi Hatao** were the main objectives of this plan.	5.7%	3.3%
Fifth Plan (1974-79)	• DP Dhar formulated it. • Removal of poverty and attainment of self reliance.	4.4%	4.8%
Janta Party came into power and ended the Fifth Plan one year before in 1978 and formulated the Sixth Plan (1978-83). The Sixth Plan was a **Rolling Plan** (Gunar Myrdal).			

Plan	Emphasis of Plan	Growth Rate	
		Target	Achieved
Sixth Plan (1980-85)	• Removal of poverty through strengthening of infrastructure for both agriculture and industry, involved people's participation at local level.	5.2%	5.7%
Seventh Plan (1985-90)	• Food, work and productivity were the main objectives of this plan.	5.0%	6.0%
Eighth Plan could not take-off due to fast changing in political situations at the Centre. Therefore, from 1990-92, Annual Plans were formulated.			
Eighth Plan (1992-97) (Based on Liberali-sation, Privatisation and Globalisation Model or Narsimham Mohan Model)	• To provide a new dynamism to the economy and improve life quality of the common man. • The planning became indicative and facilitative.	5.6%	6.8%
Ninth Plan (1997-2002)	• Growth with social justice and equality. • The recession in international economy was held and responsible for the failure of the Ninth Plan.	6.5%	5.4%
Tenth Plan (2002-2007)	• It targetted a GDP growth rate of 8% per annum. • The plan set certain equity-related social and monitorable targets with the aim to achieve overall well-being of individuals. • MTA of 11th Plan revised it to 8.1%.	8.1%	7.7%
Eleventh Plan (2007-2012)	• Towards faster and more inclusive growth, increasing the growth rate in agriculture, industry and services to 4.1%, 10% and 9%, respectively.	9%	8.2%
Twelfth Plan (2012-2017)	• Towards faster, sustainable and inclusive growth, increasing the growth rate in agriculture, industry and services to 4%, 9.6% and 10% respectively.	9 – 9.5%	

Public Finanace & Taxation

S.No.	Year of Appointment	Chairman	Operational Period
1.	1951	K.C.Niyogi	1952-57
2.	1952	K.Santhanam	1957-62
3.	1960	A.K. Chanda	1962-66
4.	1964	P.V. Rajamannar	1966-69
5.	1968	Mahavir Tyagi	1969-74
6.	1972	K.B.N. Reddy	1974-79
7.	1977	J.M. Shellat	1979-84
8.	1983	Y.B. Chawan	1984-89
9.	1987	N.K.P. Salve	1989-95
10.	1992	K.C. Pant	1995-00
11.	1998	A.M. Khusro	2000-05
12.	2002	C. Rangarajan	2005-10
13.	2007	Dr. Vijay L. Kelkar	2010-15
14.	2012	Dr. Y.V. Reddy	2015 - 2020
15.	2017	N.K. Singh	2020-2025

Indian Tax Structure

Direct Tax : The term direct tax generally means a tax paid directly to the government by the persons on whom it is imposed.

Indirect Tax : An indirect tax is a tax collected by an intermediary from the person who bears the ultimate economic burden of the tax.

- The Government of India earns maximum from **Corporate Income Tax.**

Direct Tax	Indirect Tax
Income Tax	Sales Tax or VAT
Corporation Tax	Customs Duty
Capital Gain Tax	Insurance Premium Tax
Stamp Duty	Excise Duties
Land Tax	
Estate Duty	Landfill Tax
Wealth Tax	Aggregates Levy
Petroleum	Climate Change Levy
Revenue Tax	
Inheritance Tax	Goods and Services Tax

Important Committees for Tax Reforms

Year	Committee
1956	Nicholas Kaldor Committee
1971	K.N. Wanchoo Committee
1981	L.K. Jha Committee
1991	Raja J. Chelliah Committee
2001	Parthasarthy Scheme Committee
2002	Vijay Kelkar Committee
2003	M. Govinda Rao Committee

Do You Know?

- Annual Tax on wealth was introduced in 1957 on the recommendations of **Kaldor Committee.**
- *Gift Tax* was first introduced in 1958, which was later abolished with effect from Oct. 1,1998.
- The easiest way to know the tax burden is tax-GDP ratio. In 2005-06 tax-GDP ratio was 10.5%.
- The States have exclusive control over the excise duties on Alcohol and Narcotics.
- Fiscal Responsibility and Budget Management (FRBM) Act, 2003 came into force in July, 2004, It mandates the government to eliminate revenue deficits by March, 2009.
- Haryana is the first State to introduce VAT in 2003.
- Sales Tax VAT is a State subject i.e., it is in the State List of the seventh schedule of the Constitution.

INCLUSIVE DEVELOPMENT

Human Development Index (HDI)

HDI measure was given by Pakistani Nobel Prize Winner Economist, Mehbub-ul-Haq

Estimates/Causes

- Measured by Human Development Index (HDI), published by UNDP since 1990.
- *Three dimensions*
  1. Life expectancy at birth rate;
  2. Education Index comprising means year of schooling and expected year of schooling;
  3. GNI per capita (PPPUS $) Index.

POVERTY

Estimates/Causes

- **Main Reasons for Rural Poverty**

  Rapid population growth, lack of capital, lack of alternate employment other than agriculture, illiteracy and lack of proper implementation of PDS.
- **Main Reasons for Urban Poverty**

  Migration from rural areas, lack of skilled labour, lack of housing facilities, limited job opportunities in cities.
- Based on **2400 calories** (rural) and **2100 calories** (urban) and monthly per capita consumption expenditure of ₹ 356 (rural) and 538 (urban), Planning Commission estimated poverty ratio in India in 2004-05 was 27.5%.
- The poverty ratio or the number of poor as a percentage of total population in India for 2004-05 estimated at 37.2% according to the Suresh Tendulkar Committee.

Programme/Measure	Year of Launch
Employment Guarantee Scheme	1972-73
Drought Prone Area Programme	1973-74
Twenty Point Programme	1975
Desert Development Programme	1977-78
Integrated Rural Development Programme	1980
National Rural Employment Programme	1980
Jawahar Rozgar Yojana	1989
MPLAD Programme	1993

Programme/Measure	Year of Launch
Rural Landless Employment Guarantee Programme	1993
Swarna Jayanti Shahri Rozgar Yojana	1997
Swarna Jayanti Gram Swarozgar Yojana	1999
Indira Awaas Yojana	1999
Pradhanmantri Gramodaya Yojana	2000
Pradhan Mantri Gram Sadak Yojana	2000
Sampoorna Grameen Rozgar Yojana	2001
Bharat Nirman	2005
Jawaharlal Nehru National Urban Renewal Mission	2005
Mahatma Gandhi National Rural Employment Programme	2006
Prime Minister Employment Generation Programme	2008
Affordable housing in Partnership	2009
Rajeev Awaas Yojana	2010
Pradhan Mantri Adarsh Gram Yojana	2010
National Rural livelihood Mission	2011
Pradhan Mantri Jan Dhan Yojana	2014
Pradhan Mantri Suraksha Bima Yojana	2015

Employment

A person, working 8 hours a day for 273 days of the year is regarded as employed as the main worker.

Estimates/Causes

Since 1973 on the recommendation of **B Bhagwati Committee,** three estimates of unemployment have been brought about by Planning Commission, *viz*

1. **Usual Principal Status** (*Also called Open Unemployment*) According to the NSSO, 66th Round (2009-10), rural and urban unemployment were 2% and 4%, respectively.
2. **Current Weekly Status** On this basis, the unemployment in 2009-10 in rural and urban areas were 3% and 4%, respectively.
3. **Current Daily Status** The most comprehensive measure on this basis, the unemployment for rural and urban areas were 7% and 6%, respectively (2009-10).

Women Empowerment and Child Development

Programme/Measure	Year	Programme/Measure	Year
ICDS	1975	Ujjwala	2007
Mid-Day Meal Scheme	1995	Dhanlaxmi	2008
Swadhar	1995	Gender Budgeting	2009
Swayam Sidha	2001	Integrated Child Protection Scheme	2009-10
SSA	2001	Sabla Scheme	2010
Support to Training and Employment Programme for Women (STEP)	2003-04	National Mission for Empowerment of Women	2010
		Bal Bandu Scheme	2011
		Beti Padhao Beti Bachao	2015

The theme of the Human Development Report-2011 is *'Sustainability and Equity'*- A better future for all.

INDUSTRIES

Industrial Policies

- Industrial Policies were launched in 1948, 1956, 1977, 1980 and 1991.
- Industrial Policy 1956 is called **'Economic Constitution of India'** and gave public sector the strategic edge.
- Industrial Policy 1991 opened up the economy.
- The main aims were:
  (*a*) to end license-permitraj;
  (*b*) to integrate Indian economy with the outer world;
  (*c*) to remove restrictions on FDI and
  (*d*) to reform public sectors.

Public Sector Enterprises (PSEs)

- Industries requiring compulsory licensing
  (*a*) distillation and brewing of alcoholic drinks;
  (*b*) cigar and cigarettes of tobacco;
  (*c*) electronic aerospace and defence equipment;
  (*d*) industrial explosives;
  (*e*) specific hazardous chemicals.
- Areas reserved for public sector are
  (*a*) atomic energy-production, separation and enrichment of fissionable materials; and
  (*b*) railways.
- Present policy on PSEs is to
  (*a*) not to privatize profit-making companies and to modernize and revive sick companies;
  (*b*) not to bring government stake in PSEs below 51%;
  (*c*) to adopt initial public offering route to disinvestment.
- There are **249 Central PSEs** as on 31st March, 2010.

Navratnas and Maharatnas

- The concept of Navratnas were started in 1997. At present there are **16 Navratnas** and **65 Miniratnas.**
- **Maharatnas** were started in 2009. **Five Maharatnas** ONGC, SAIL, IOC, NTPC and Coal India Ltd.
- **Navratnas** Bharat Electronics Ltd, BHEL, BPCL, GAIL (India) Ltd, HAL, HPCL, MTNL, NALCO, National Mineral Development Corporation, Nevyeli Lignite Company Ltd, Oil India Ltd, Power Finance Company Ltd, Power Grid Corporation of India Ltd, Rashtriya Ispat Nigam Ltd, Rural Electrification Corporation Ltd and Shipping Corporation of India Ltd.

Small Scale Industry

- A new thrust to small scale industry, given in Industrial Policy of 1977.
- MSMED Act, 2006 and new definition.
- Contributes 8% to GDP, 45% to all manufactures and 40% to exports.
- According to the 4th Census (2009) of SSIs, 67% of the MSME are in manufacturing and 33% are in services sector.

Committees on Various Sectors of Indian Economy

AC Shah Committee	Non-Banking Financial Company
Bimal Jalan Committee	Market Infrastructure Instruments
Malegam Committee	Functioning of Micro Finance
Birla Committee	Corporate Governance
Kirith Parikh Committee	Rationalization of Petroleum Product Prices
Chaturvedi Committee	Improving National Highways in India
S R Hashim Committee	Urban Poverty
Abhijit Sen	Wholesale Price Index
C Rangarajan	Services Price Index
Abid Hussain Committee	Development of Capital Markets
Damodaran Committee	Customer Service in Banks
Khandelwal Committee	Human Resource in Commercial Banks
Patii Committee	Corporate Debt
VK Sharma Committee	Credit to Marginal Farmers
Sarangi Committee	Non-Performing Assets
Khanna Committee	Regional Rural Banks
Dantawala Committee	Lead Bank Scheme
Gadgil Committee	Financial Inclusion

BANKING AND FINANCE

Banking in India

- **Bank of Hindustan** was the first bank, established in India in 1770.
- First bank with limited liability managed by an **Indian Board** was the Oudh Commercial Bank in 1881.
- First purely Indian bank is the **Punjab National Bank (1894).**
- A step towards **'social banking'** was taken with the nationalization of 14 **Commercial Banks** on 19 July, 1969. Six more banks were nationalized on 1980, total number of nationalized banks are 27.
- With the merger of Bank of Rajasthan with the ICICI Bank, the number of old private sector banks is now reduced, 14.
- After the merger of State Bank of Saurashtra and State Bank of Indore with the SBI, the number of Associates of SBI are 6.

THE RBI AND CREDIT CONTROL

Quantitative/General Credit Control

It is used to control the volume of credit, and indirectly to control the inflationary and deflationary pressures. These are

1. Cash Reserve Ratio
2. Statutory Liquidity Ratio (SLR)
3. Repo Rate
4. Reverse Repo Rate
5. Bank Rate

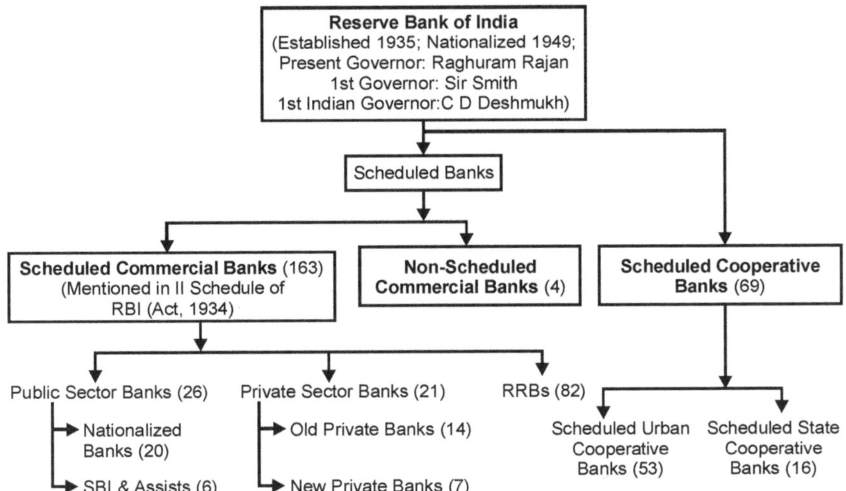

Functions of the RBI

The functions of the RBI, today can be categorized as follows :

- Monetary Policy
- Regulation and supervision of the banking and non-banking financial institutions, including credit information companies
- Debt and cash management for Centre and State Governments
- Management of foreign exchange reserves
- Foreign exchange management—current and capita account management
- Banker's banks
- Banker to the Centre and State Governments
- Oversight of the payment and settlement systems
- Currency management
- Development role
- Research and statistics

POLICY RATES & RESERVE RATIOS

Bank Rate	7.75%
Repo Rate	6.75%
Reverse Repo Rate	5.75%
Cash Reserve Ratio (CRR)	4.00%
Statutory Liquidity Ratio (SLR)	21.5%
Base Rate	9.70% - 10.00%
Marginal Standing Facility Rate	7.75%

Indian Banks Operating Abroad

- 22 Indian banks (6 Private and 16 Public) operate overseas in 52 countries.
- SBI has the largest network of foreign offices followed by Bank of Baroda.
- Among private sector banks, ICICI Bank has the largest foreign presence.

AGRICULTURE

Green Revolution is associated with the use of HYVS (High Yielding Variety Seeds}, chemical fertilizers and new technology which led to a revolutionary results in agriculture production during the middle of 1960.

The term Green Revolution was given by American Scientist **Dr William Gande.**

Agriculture Credit

- Institutional credit covers cooperative societies and banks, commercial banks, **RRBs** and **NABARD.**
- Lead Bank Scheme (1969) is an area approach to credit.
- Service area approach to credit was adopted in 1988.
- NABARD as an apex agricultural bank was set up in 1982.

Importance of Agriculture

- Contributes 14.2% to the GDP (2010-11).
- Provides employment 58 per cent.

  Contribution 10.2% to the exports.

Important Committees

Committees	Appointed For
Ghosh Committee	Bank frauds
Goiporia Committee	Bank customer services
Omkar Goswami Committee	Industrial sickness and corporate re-structuring
Jilani Committee	Internal control and Inspection/Audit System in Banks
Janakiraman Committee	Securities transactions of the banks and financial institutions
Malhotra Committee	insurance sector reforms
Dr. Mehta Committee	Integrated Rural Development Programme
Nadkarni Committee	Trading in the Public Sector Bonds and units of mutual funds
Ist Narasimham Committee	Financial/Banking sector reforms
IInd Narasimham Committee	Financial/Banking sector reforms
Nayak Committee	Credit to small scale industry sector
W.S. Saraf Committee	Technology issue in the banking industry
Sodhani Committee	NRI investment and forex markets
S.S. Tarapore Committee	Capital Account Convertibility
Verma Committee	Problems of weak banks
R. V. Gupta Committee	Agriculture credit through commerical banks
J. J. Irani Committee	Company Reforms
S. S. Kohli Committee	Rehabilitation of sick small scale industries

Committees	Appointed For
Y. V. Reddy Committee	Reforms in small savings
Raja Chelliah Committee	Tax Reforms
Raghavan Committee	Competition Law
Suma Verma Committee	to update, and revise the Banking Ombudsman scheme 2008
Demodran Committee	on improvement of customer services in banks
Shri M. Narasimham Committee	on Banking Sector Reforms
Shri Raghuram Rajan Committee	On Financial Sector Reforms
Shri B. Mahapatra Committee	to review the existing prudential guidelines on restructuring of advances by banks/ financial institution
Shri Aditya Puri Committee	Dissemination of Credit Information
Shri K.U.B. Rao Committee	Recommended aligning gold import regulations
K.M Chandrasekhar committee	For rationalization of foreign investment norms
Shri Pulak Kumar Sinha Committe	to study the feasibility of Aadhaar as an additional factor for authentication of card present transactions
Mukul Mudgal Committe	looking into US giant Walmart's lobbying activities to enter India
MBN Rao Committee	To prepare the blueprint of India's first women'sbank
Arvind Mayaram Committee	For giving clear definitions to Foreign Direct Investment (FDI) and Foreign Institutional Investment (FII)

Important Abbreviations

ITEs : Intra-Group Transactions and Exposures

LCR : Liquidity Coverage Ratio

NSFR : Net Stable Funding Ratio

LRMT : Liquidity risk monitoring tools

CBS : Core Banking Solution

DEAF : Depositor Education and Awareness Fund

CRAR : Capital to Risk-weighted Assets Ratio

ECB : External Commercial Borrowings

SWIFT : Society for Worldwisde Interbank Financial Telecommunication

FSLRC : Financial Sector Legislative REforms Commission

MIBOR : Mumbai Inter-Bank Offer Rate

LIBOR : London Inter-Bank Offer Rate

LAF : Liquidity Adjustment Facility

GIRO : Government Internal Revenue Order

EEFC : Exchange Earner's Foreign Currency

FRBMA : Fiscal Responsibility and Budget Management Act.

Glossary of Economics' Terms

- **Assets** Property of any kind.
- **Balance of Trade** (or Payment) The difference between the exports and imports of two countries in trade with each other is called balance of payment. If the difference is positive the Balance of Payment (BoP) is called favourable and if negative it is called unfavourable.
- **Balance Sheet** It is a statement of accounts, generally of a business concern, prepared at the end of a year, showing debits and credits under broad heads, to find out the profit and loss position.
- **Banker's Cheque** A cheque by one bank to another.
- **Bank Rate** It is the rate of interest charged by the Reserve Bank of India for lending money to Commercial Banks.
- **Barter** To trade by exchanging one commodity for another.
- **Bearer** This term on cheques and bills denotes that any person holding the same, has the same right in respect of it, as the person who issued it.
- **Black Money** It means unaccounted money, concealed income and undisclosed wealth. In order to evade taxes some people falsify their account and do not record all transactions in their books. The money which thus remains unaccounted for, is called the Black Money.
- **Bilateral Monopoly** Existence of single buyer and single seller.
- **Bond** A legal agreement to pay a certain sum of money (called principal) at some future date and carrying a fixed rate of interest.
- **Budget** An estimate of expected revenues and expenditure for a given period, usually a year, item by item.
- **Budget Deficit** When the expenditure of the government exceeds the revenue, the balance between the two is the budget deficit.
- **Bulls** Speculators in the stock markets who buy goods, in some cases without money to pay with, anticipating that prices will go up.
- **Buyer's Market** An area in which the supply of certain goods exceeds the demands so that purchasers can drive hard bargains.
- **Call Money** Loan made for a very short period. It carries a low rate of interest.
- **Commercial Banks** Financial institutions that create credit accept deposits, give loans and perform other financial functions. They create credit by creating deposits on the basis of their cash reserve ratio.
- **Deflation** It is a state in monetary market when money in circulation has decreased and is characterized by low prices, unemployment, etc.
- **Depreciation** Reduction in the value of fixed assets due to wear and tear.
- **Devaluation** Official reduction in the foreign value of domestic currency. It is done to encourage the country's exports and discourage imports.
- **Direct Tax** Taxes that are directly borne by the person on whom it was initially fixed. e.g., Personal income tax.
- **Dividend** Earning of stock paid to shareholders.
- **Dumping** Sale of a commodity at different prices in different markets, lower price being charged in a market where demand is relatively elastic.
- **Exchange Rate** The rate at which central banks will exchange one country's currency for another.
- **Excise Duty Tax** Imposed on the manufacture, sale and consumption of various commodities, such as taxes on textiles, cloth, liquor, etc.

- **Fiscal Policy** Government's expenditure and Tax Policy.
- **Gross Domestic Product** (*GDP*) A measure of the total flow of goods and services produced by the economy over a specific time period, normally a year. It is obtained by valuing output of goods and services at market prices and then aggregating.
- **Repo Rate** The rate at which banks borrow from RBI. It injects liquidity into the market.
- **Indirect Taxes** Taxes levied on goods purchased by the consumer for which the taxpayer's liabilities varies in proportion to the quantity of particular goods purchased or sold.
- **Inflation** A sustained and appreciable increase in the price level over a considerable period of time.
- **Monopoly** Single seller selling single product.
- **Monopolistic Competition** Existence of too many sellers selling differentiated products.
- **Monopsony** Single buyer buying product being unique.
- **Oligopoly** Existence of few sellers and few products. Price war is a common feature.
- **Perfect Competition** Existence of too many sellers selling homogeneous product.
- **Reverse Repo Rate** The rate at which RBI borrows from banks for a short-term. It withdraws liquidity into the market.

PRADHAN MANTRI JAN DHAN YOJANA (PMJDY)

1. Hon'ble Prime Minister will launch the National Mission on Financial Inclusion named as **Pradhan Mantri Jan Dhan Yojana** (PMJDY) on 28th August, 2014.
2. The mission will be implemented in two phases.
3. Phase - I form 15th August 2014 to 14th August 2015

   (i) Universal access to banking facilities for all households across the country through as bank branck or a fixed point Business Correspondent (BC) within a reasonable distance

   (ii) To cover all households with atleast one Basic Banking Account with Rupay Debit card having inbuilt accident insurance cover of ₹1 lakh. Further an overdraft facility upto ₹ 5000 will also be permitted to Adhaar enabled accounts after satisfactory operation in the account for 6 month.

   (iii) Financial literacy programme which aims to take financial literacy upto village level.

   (iv) The Mission also envisages expansion of Direct Benefit Transfer under various Government Schemes through bank accounts of the beneficiaries of

   (v) The issuance of Kisan Credit Card (KCC) as RuPay Kisan Card is also proposed to be covered under the plan.
4. Phase-II from 15tyh August, 2015 to 14th August 2018

   (i) Providing micro-insurance to the people

   (ii) Unorganised sector Pension schemes like Swavalamban through the Business correspondents
5. The major shift in this programme is that households are being targeted instead of villages as targeted earlier. Moreover both rural and urban areas are being covered this time as aginst only rural areas targeted earlier. The present plan pursues digital financial inclusion with special emphasis on monitoring by a Mission headed by the Finance Minister.
6. Hon'ble Prime Minister will launch the Yojana at a National level function at 4.00 PM in Delhi on 28th August ,2014. Besides the launch function at Delhi, simultaneous launch functions of the Yojana will also be held in Capitals and other major centres of the State and at all district Headquarters. Besides, camps would also be organized in the area allotted to branches of the banks. At State level, Chief Ministers of States have been requested to launch the Yojana.

Objective of "Pradhan Mantri Jan-Dhan Yojana (PMJDY)" is ensuring access to various financial services like availability of basic savings bank account, access to need based credit, remittances facility, insurance and pension to the excluded sections i.e. weaker sections & low income groups. This deep penetration at affordable cost is possible only with effective use of technology.

PMJDY is a National Mission on Financial Inclusion encompassing an integrated approach to bring about comprehensive financial inclusion of all the households in the country. Theplan envisages universal access to banking facilities with at least one basic banking account for every household, financial literacy, access to credit, insurance and pension facility. In addition, the beneficiaries would get RuPay Debit card having inbuilt accident insurance cover of ₹ 1 lakh. The plan also envisages channeling all Government benefits (from Centre/ State/ Local Body) to the beneficiaries accounts and pushing the Direct Benefits Transfer (DBT) scheme of the Union Government. The technological issues like poor connectivity, on-line transactions will be addressed. Mobile transactions through telecom operators and their established centres as Cash Out Points are also planned to be used for Financial Inclusion under the Scheme. Also an effort is being made to reach out to the youth of this country to participate in this Mission Mode Programme.

■ ■

SCIENCE AND TECHNOLOGY

SPACE RESEARCH

INDIA'S SPACE PROGRAMME

- Space-includes air and atmosphere.
- Outer space-outside the atmosphere.
- Indian's space progrmame launched in 1962.
- ISRO was established in 1969, with its H.Q. at Banglore. *ISRO provides the research base for the development of space technology.*
- Space commission was set-up in 1972.
- Thumba Equatorial Rocket Launching station near Thiruvanthapuram in Kerala was set-up in 1963 for launching facilities.
- Sriharikota Range (SHAR) is a satellite launching station set up in Sriharikota in Andhra Pradesh. SHAR has been renamed as **Satish Dhawan Space Centre**.
- The first Indian satellite Aryabhatta was launched on Apr. 19, 1975 from Baikanpur (erstwhile USSR).
- The first Indian Remote Sensing Satellite was launched on Mar 17, 1988.

GEO STATIONARY SATELLITE (GSS) OR GEO SYNCHRONOUS SATELLITE

- It orbits the earth above the equator at height of about 36000 km taking same time to complete one orbit taken by earth to spin once on its axis. Therefore a GSS is fixed in space in relation to the earth and can cover a fixed area of surface of earth.
- It normally covers a little over 1/3rd surface of earth for communication.

INSAT system (Indian National Satellite)

- It is the communication satellite of India and originally consider two generations.
- It is joint venture of DOS (Deptt. of Space) and DOT, IMD (India Metrological Department), D.D. (Door-Darshan) and AIR (All India Radio).

INVENTIONS AND DISCOVERIES

Invention	Year	Inventor	Country
Aeroplane	1903	Orville and W. Wright	U.S.A.
Bakelite	1907	L.H. Baekeland	Belgium
Ball-point pen	1888	John J. Loud	U.S.A.
Barometer	1644	E.Torricelli	Italy
Barometer, Aneriod	1799	W.J.Cante	Italy
Bicycle	1839	K. Macmillan	Britain

Invention	Year	Inventor	Country
Bicycle tyre (air)	1888	J.B. Dunlop	Britain
Calculating Machine	1642	Blaise Pascal	France
Celluloid	1861	A. Parker	Britain
Centigrade Scale	1742	A. Celsius	France
Chloroform	1831	E.Soberran	France
Cine camera	1889	Wm. Friese-Greene	Britain
Cinema	1895	A.L. and J. Lumiere	France
Circulation of blood	1628	William Harvey	England
Clock (mechanical)	1725	Hsing and Ling-Tsan	China
Clock (pendulum)	1657	Christian Huygens	Holland
Diesel Engine	1892	Rudolf Diesel	Germany
Dynamite	1867	Alfred Nobel	Sweden
Dynamo (principle)	1831	Michael Faraday	England
Dynamo (in practice)	1860	Picinotti	Italy
Electric iron	1882	H.W. Seeley	U.S.A.
Electric lamp	1879	Thomas Alva Edison	U.S.A.
Electric motor	1834	Moritz Jacobi	Russia
Evolution, theory of	1858	Charles Darwin	England
Film sound	1923	Dr. Le de Forest	U.S.A.
Fountain pen	1884	L.E. Waterman	U.S.A.
Glider	1853	Sir Gerorge Cayley	England
Gramophone	1878	Thomas Alva Edison	U.S.A.
Insulin	1923	Sir Grederick Banting	Canada
Jet engine	1937	Sir Frank Whittle	England
Lift	1852	E.G. Otis	U.S.A.
Lightning conductor	1752	Benjamin Franklin	U.S.A.
Locomotive, steam	1804	Richard Trevithic	England
Machine gun	1861	Richard Gatling	U.S.A.
Match, safety	1855	J.E.Lundstrom	Sweden
Microphone	1878	David Hughes	U.S.A.
Microscope	1590	Z. Janssen	Holland
Motor car, petrol	1885	Karl Benz	Germany
Motorcycle	1884	Edward Butler	England
Parachute	1797	A.J.Garnerin	France
Penicillin	1928	Alexander Fleming	England
Photography (film)	1888	Hohn Carbutt	U.S.A.
Piano	1711	Cristofori	Italy
Radar	1922	Taylor and Young	U.S.A.
Radium	1898	Marie & Pierre Curie	France

Invention	Year	Inventor	Country
Radio	1901	Guglielmo Marconi	Italy
Rayon	1883	Sir Hoseph Swann	England
Refrigerator	1851	James Harrison	Scotland
Revolver	1835	Samuel Colt	U.S.A.
Rubber (vulcanised)	1841	Charles Goodyear	U.S.A.
Safety lamp	1816	Sir Humphry Davy	England
Safety pin	1849	William Hurst	U.S.A.
Ship, steam	1775	J.C.Perier	France
Ship, turbine	1894	Sir Charles Parsons	Britain
Steam engine	1639	Thomas Savery	Britain
Submarine	1776	David Bushnell	U.S.A.
Telegraph code	1837	Samuel F.B. Morse	U.S.A.
Thermometer	1608	Hans Lippershey	Netherlands
Television	1926	John Logie Baird	Scotland
Telescope	1593	Galileo	Italy
Typewriter	1864	Mitterhofer	Austria
Valve, radio	1904	Sir J.A. Fleming	Britain
Watch	1791	A.L. Breguet	France
X-ray	1895	Wilhelm Roentgen	Germany

VARIOUS SCIENCES

Science	Related with
Acoustics	Study of sound (or science of sound)
Aerodynamics	that deals with the motion of air and other gases.
Aeronautics	Science or art of flight.
Agronomy	Science of soil management and production of field crops.
Agrostolgy	Study of grasses.
Anatomy	Science dealing with structure of animals, plants or human body.
Anthropology	Science dealing with the origins, physical and cultural development of mankind.
Archaeology	Study of antiquities.
Astrology	Ancient art of predicting the course of human destinies with the help of indications deduced from position and movement of the heavenly bodies.
Astronautics	Science of Space travel.
Astronomy	Study of heavenly bodies.

Science	Related with
Astrophysics	Branch of astronomy concerned with the physical nature of heavenly bodies.
Bacteriology	Study of Bacteria.
Biochemistry	Study of chemical processes of living things.
Biology	Study of living things.
Biometry	Application of mathematics to the study of living things.
Bionomics	Study of the relation of an organism to its environment.
Botany	Study of plants.
Ceramics	Art and technology of making objects from clay, etc.
Chemotherapy	Treatment of diseases using chemical substances.
Conchology	Branch of zoology dealing with the shells of molluscs.
Cosmology	Study of universe as a whole and of its form, nature etc.
Cryptography	Study of Ciphers (secret writings)
Cryogenics	Science dealing with the production, control and application of very low temperatures.
Cytology	Study of cells, especially their formation, structure and functions.
Dactylography	Study of finger prints for the purpose of identification.
Ecology	Study of the relation of animals and plants to their surroundings, animate and inanimate.
Economics	Science dealing with the production, distribution and consumption of goods and services.
Embryology	Study of development of embryos.
Entomology	Study of insects.
Epidemiology	Branch of medicine dealing with epidemic diseases.
Epigraphy	Study of inscriptions.
Ethology	Study of animal behaviour.
Genealogy	Study of family origins and history.
Genesiology	Science of generation.
Genetics	Branch of biology dealing with the phenomena of heredity and the laws governing it.
Geography	Development of science of the earth's surface, physical features, climate, population etc.
Geology	Science that deals with the physical history of the earth.
Geomorphology	Study of the characteristics, origin and development of landforms.

Science	Related with
Gerontology	Study of old age, its phenomena, diseases etc.
Histology	Study of tissues.
Horticulture	Cultivation of flowers, fruits, vegetables and ornamental plants.
Metallurgy	Process of extracting metals from their ores.
Meteorology	Science of the atmosphere and its phenomena.
Metrology	Scientific study of weights and measures.
Microbiology	Study of minute living organisms, including bacteria, moulds, and pathogenic protozoa.
Neurology	Study of the nervous system, its functions and its disorders.
Mycology	Study of fungi and fungus diseases.
Numerology	Study of numbers.
Optics	Study of nature and properties of light.
Ornithology	Study of birds.
Osteology	Study of bones.
Paleobotany	Study of fossil plants.
Paleontology	Study of fossils.
Pathology	Study of diseases.
Phonetics	Study of speech sounds.
Phycology	Study of Algae.
Physics	Study of the properties of matter.
Physiology	Study of functioning of organs of living beings.
Pomology	Science that deals with fruits and fruit growing.
Psychology	Study of human and animal behaviour.
Radiology	Study of X-rays and radioactivity.
Rheology	Study of the deformation and flow of matter.
Scientology	Study of earthquakes.
Sociology	Study of human society.
Topography	A special description of a part or region.
Virology	Study of viruses.
Zoology	Study of animal life.

Important Facts
Lowest Freezing point
Mercury freeze at – 38.8°C. It is liquid at room temperature.
Highest melting point
Carbon melt at 3652°C (6606° F) two-thirds as hot as Sun's surface.
Rarest element
Astatine is the rarest element on Earth.
Scarest element
Rhodium is the scarest metal Just 3 tones mined every year.
Heaviest metal
Osmium. It's 33-cm^3 (13-in^3) cube weighs 640 kg.

SCIENTIFIC INSTRUMENTS AND APPLIANCES

Instrument	Use
Altimeter	It is a special type of aneroid barometer, used in measuring altitudes.
Ammeter	It is an instrument used to measure strength of an electric current.
Anemometer	It is an instrument used to measure velocity and find direction of the wind.
Audiometer	It is an instrument used to measure difference in hearing.
Barometer	It is used for measuring atmospheric pressure.
Calorimeter	It is an instrument used for measuring quantities of heat.
Chronometer	It is a clock to determine longitude of a vessel at sea.
Clinical Thermometer	It is a thermometer for measuring temperature of human body.
Colorimeter	It is an instrument used for comparing intensities of colour.
Commutator	It is an instrument used to change or reverse the direction of an electric current.
	In dynamo it is used to convert the alternating current into direct current.
Computer	It is a technical device designed to find instantaneous solutions of huge and complex calculations based on the information already fed.
Crescograph	It is an instrument used for measuring growth of plants. This was invented by an Indian, Mr. J.C. Bose, a renowned Botanist.
Cyclotron	It is an apparatus used for electromagnetic acceleration of charged atoms. It has made possible to make ordinary elements radioactive, leading to production of radioactive isotopes.
Dictaphone	It is a machine, which first records what is spoken into it and then, reproduces it in type.

Instrument	Use
Dynamo	It is a device used for converting mechanical energy into electrical energy.
Dynamometer Electro-cardiograph (ECG)	It is an instrument used for measuring electrical power. It is an instrument used for detection of electric impulses of the heart. It gives a graphic picture of heartbeats.
Electroence-phalograph (EEG)	It is an instrument used for recording of change in electric potential in various area of the brain by means of electrode on the scalp or in the brain itself.
Electrometer	It is an instrument used for measuring electricity.
Electroscope	It is an instrument used for detecting presence of electric charge.
Galvanometer	It is an instrument used for measuring electric current.
Hydrometer	It is an instrument used for measuring the relative density of liquids.
Hydroscope	It is an optical instrument used for seeing objects below the surface of water.
Hygrometer	It is an instrument used for measuring the relative humidity of the atmosphere.
Hygroscope	It is an instrument used to show the changes in atmospheric humidity.
Hypsometer	It is an instrument used to measure height above sea level. It is an apparatus used for detecting boiling point of liquid. Since boiling points of liquids have a direct relationship with atmospheric pressure and atmospheric pressure with altitude, therefore instrument may be used for determination of altitude above sea level. This instrument is generally used by the mountaineers.
Lactometer	Lactometer is an instrument for measuring the relative density of milk.
Manometer	Manometer is an instrument to measure the pressure of gases.
Mariners's Compass	It is an apparatus for determining direction, graduated to indicate 33 directions. The "N" point on the dial indicate North pole and the "S" point, South pole.
Magnetometer	It is an instrument used to compare magnetic moments and fields.
Megaphone	It is an instrument used for carrying sound to long distances.
Microphone	It is an instrument used for converting sound waves into electrical energy which is transmitted through wires and then recovered into sound in a magnified intensity.
Microscope	It is an instrument used for magnified view of very small objects.
Periscope	It is an apparatus used for viewing objects lying above the eye level of the observer and whose direct vision is obstructed. It consists of a tube bent twice at right angles and having plane mirrors at these bends inclined at angles of 45° to the tube.
Photometer	It is an instrument used for comparing luminous intensity of the sources of light.

Instrument	Use
Pyknometer	It is an instrument used to measure the density and coefficient of expansion of liquid.
Pyrheliometer	It is an instrument used for measuring solar radiations.
Pyrometers	These are the thermometers used to measure high temperature.
Radar	It is used for detecting and finding range of moving objects by transmitting beams of radio waves.
Radio micrometer	It is an instrument for measuring heat radiations.
Rain gauge	It is an instrument used for measuring rainfall.
Refractometer	It is an instrument used to measure refractive index of a substance.
Resistance thermometer	It is used for determining electrical resistance of conductor.
Salinometer	It is a type of hydrometer used to determine con-centration of salt solutions by measuring their densities.
Seismograph	It is an instrument used for recording intensity and origin of earthquake shocks.
Sextant	It is an instrument used for measurement of angular distances between two objects.
Sphygmomanometer	It is an apparatus used for measuring blood pressure.
Stereoscope	It is an optical device used to see two dimensional pictures as having depth and solidity.
Stethoscope	It is a medical instrument used for hearing and analysing the sound of heart and lungs.
Tape recorder	It is an apparatus which records and reproduces sound by using magnetic tapes.
Telephone	It is an apparatus used for transmission of sound.
Teleprinter	It is a communication medium for automatic sending, receiving and printing of telegraphic messages from distant places.
Telescope	It is an instrument used for viewing distant objects as magnified.
Television	It is an instrument used for transmitting visible moving images by means of wireless makes.
Thermometer	It is an instrument used to measure the temperature.
Thermostat	It is an automatic device used for regulating constant temperatures.
Transistor	It is a small device which may be used to amplify current and perform other functions usually performed by a thermionic value.
Viscometer	It is an instrument used for measuring viscosity i.e., property of resistance of a fluid to relative motion within itself.
Voltmeter	It is an instrument used to measure potential difference between two points.

ELEMENTS, SYMBOLS AND ATOMIC NUMBERS

Name	Symbol	Atomic Number	Name	Symbol	Atomic Number
Hydrogen	H	1	Iron (Ferum)	Fe	26
Helium	He	2	Cobalt	Co	27
Lithium	Li	3	Nickel	Ni	28
Beryllium	Be	4	Copper (Cuprum)	Cu	29
Boron	B	5	Zinc	Zn	30
Carbon	C	6	Germenium	Ge	32
Nitrogen	N	7	Bromine	Br	35
Oxygen	O	8	Krypton	Kr	36
Flourine	F	9	Zirconium	Zr	40
Neon	Ne	10	Silver	Ag	47
Sodium (Natrium)	Na	11	Tin (Stannum)	Sn	50
Magnesium	Mg	12	Antimony (Stabnium)	Sb	51
Aluminium	Al	13	Iodine	I	53
Silicon	Si	14	Barium	Ba	56
Phosphorous	P	15	Gold (Aurum)	Au	79
Sulphur	S	16	Mercury (Hydragerm)	Hg	80
Chlorine	Cl	17	Lead (Plumbum)	Pb	82
Argon	Ar	18	Bismuth	Bi	83
Potassium (Kalium)	K	19	Radium	Ra	88
Calcium	Ca	20	Thorium	Th	90
Titanium	Ti	22	Uranium	U	92
Vanadium	V	23	Plutonium	Pu	94
Chromium	Cr	24	Curium	Cm	96
Manganese	Mn	25			

COMMON AND CHEMICAL NAMES OF SOME COMPOUNDS

Common Name	Chemical Name	Chemical Formulae
Dry Ice	Solid Carbondioxide	CO_2
Slaked Lime	Calcium Hydroxide	$Ca(OH)_2$
Bleaching Powder	Calcium Oxychloride	$CaOCl_2$
Nausadar	Ammonium Chloride	NH_4Cl
Caustic Soda	Sodium Hydroxide	NaOH
Rock Salt	Sodium Chloride	NaCl

Common Name	Chemical Name	Chemical Formulae
Caustic Potash	Potassium Hydroxide	KOH
Potash Alum	Potassium Aluminium Sulphate	$K_2SO_4.\ Al_2(SO_4)_3.24H_2O$
Epsom	Magnesium sulphate	$MgSO_4.7H_2O$
Quick Lime	Calcium Oxide	CaO
Plaster of Paris	Calcium Sulphate	$(CaSO_4)1/2H_2O$
Gypsum	Calcium Sulphate	$CaSO_4.2H_2O$
Green Vitriol	Ferrous Sulphate	$FeSO_4.7H_2O$
Mohr's Salt	Ammonium Ferrous Sulphate	$FeSO_4(NH_4)_2SO_4.6H_2O$
Blue Vitriol	Copper Sulphate	$CuSO_4.5H_2O$
White Vitriol	Zinc Sulphate	$ZnSO_4.7H_2O$
Marsh Gas	Methane	CH_4
Vinegar	Acetic Acid	CH_3COOH
Potash Ash	Potassium Carbonate	K_2CO_3
Hypo	Sodium Thiosulphate	$Na_2S_2O_3.5H_2O$
Baking Powder	Sodium Bicarbonate	$NaHCO_3$
Washing Soda	Sodium Carbonate	$Na_2CO_3.10H_2O$
Magnesia	Magnesium Oxide	MgO
Chalk (Marble)	Calcium Carbonate	$CaCO_3$
Lunar Caustic	Silver Nitrate	$AgNO_3$
Laughing Gas	Nitrous Oxide	N_2O
Chloroform	Trichloro Methane	$CHCl_3$
Vermelium	Mercuric Sulphide	HgS
Borax	Borax	$Na_2B_4O_7.10H_2O$
Alcohol	Ethyl Alcohol	$C_2H_5\ OH$
Sugar	Sucrose	$C_{12}H_{22}\ O_{11}$
Heavy Water	Duterium Oxide	D_2O
Globar's Salt	Sodium Sulphate	$Na_2SO_4.10H_2O$
T.N.T.	Tri Nitrotoluene	$C_6H_2CH_3(NO_2)_3$
Calomel	Mercurous Chloride	$HgCl$
Sand	Silicon Oxide	SiO_2

SOME IMPORTANT ALLOYS

Name	Composition	Use
Brass	Cu (60 to 80%), Zn(40 to20%)	For making household utencils
Bornze	Cu(75 to 90%), Sn (25 to 10%)	For making coins, idols, utencils
German Silver	Cu(60%), Zn (25%), Ni(15%)	For making utencils
Magnelium	Mg (5%), Al(95%)	For making aircraft frame

Name	Composition	Use
Rolled Gold	Cu(90%), Ni(10%)	For making cheap ornaments
Monel metal	Cu(70%), Ni(30%)	For making alkali resistant containers
Bell metals	Cu(80%), Sn(20%)	For making bells
Gun metal	Cu (85%), Zn (10%), Sn(5%)	Used for engineering purpose
Solder	Sn (50–75%), Pb(50-25%)	Soldering of metals
Duralium	Al (95%), Cu(4%), Mg(0.5%), Mn(0.5%)	In aircraft manufacturing
Steel	Fe(98%), C(2%)	For making nails, screws, bridges
Stainless	Fe(82%) Cr, Ni(18%) Steel	For making cooking utencils, knives
* *An alloy is a mixture of two or more metals*		

SOME IMPORTANT FACTS OF HUMAN BODY

Length of alimentary canal	Approximately 8 metres
BMR (Basal metabolic rate)	1600 K.Cal/day
Number of cells in body	75 trillion
Longest bone	Femur (thigh bone)
Smallest bone	Ear ossicle, stapes
Weight of brain	1400 gms
Blood volume	6.8 litres (in 70 kg body)
Normal B.P.	120/80 mm Hg
Number of R.B.C.	**(*a*) In male :** 4.5-5.0 million/cubic mm **(*b*) In female :** 4.0-4.5 million/cubic mm
Life span of R.B.C.	120 days
Normal W.B.C. count	5000-10000/cubic mm
Life span of W.B.C.	3-4 days
D.L.C. (Differential leucocyte count)	(*a*) Basophils – 0.5-1% (*b*) Eosinophils-1-3% (*c*) Monocytes-3-8% (*d*) Neutrophils-40-70% (*e*) Lymphocytes-2-25%
Blood platelets count	2,00,000-4,00,000/cubic mm
Haemoglobin	**(*a*) In male :** 14-15.6 gm/100c.c. of blood **(*b*) In female:** 11-14 gm/100c.c. of blood
Hb content in body	500-700 gm
Universal Wood donor	O Rh-ve
Universal blood recipient	AB

Blood clotting time	2-5 minutes
Average body weight	70 kg
Normal body temperature	98.4°F or 37°C
Breathing rate	16-20/minute
Dental formula	**adult:** 2123/2123 = 32; **child:** 2120/2120 = 22 milk teeth
Number of cranial nerves	12 pairs
Number of spinal nerves	31 pairs
Largest endocrine gland	Thyroid
Gestation period	9 months (253-266 days)
Normal heart beat	72-75/minute
Largest gland	Liver
Largest muscle in the body	Gluteus maximus (Buttock muscle)
Largest smooth muscle	Uterus of pregnant woman
Smallest muscle in the body	Stapedius
Largest artery	Abdominal aorta
Largest vein	Inferior venacava
Largest W.B.C.	Monocyte
Smallest W.B.C.	Lymphocyte
Greatest regeneration power	In liver
Longest nerve	Sciatic
Longest cell	Neuron (nerve cell)
Menstrual cycle	28 days
Menopause age	45-50 years
Minimum regeneration power	in brain cells
Minimum distance for proper vision	25 cm
Type of placenta	Haemochorial (Chorioallantoic)
Pulse rate	72/minute
Volume of semen	2-4 ml/ejaculation
Normal sperm count	200-350 million/ejaculation
ESR (normal Erythrocyte sedimentation rate)	4.10 min./hour
Thinnest skin	Conjunctiva
pH of gastric juice	1.4
pH of urine	6.0
pH of blood	7.35-7.45

BLOOD

- Blood is a fluid connective tissue.
- Its quantity is 6.8 litres in man and 500 ml less in woman
- Constitutes 6–8% of body weight and has a pH of 7.4.

BLOOD CELLS

They are of 3 types :

1. **Red Blood Corpuscles (RBCs)**
    - Also called **erythrocytes,** disc-shaped, no nucleus, contains a pigment called Haemoglobin, which gives blood its red color and transports oxygen and carbon dioxide.
    - Manufactured in Red Bone marrow.
    - Life is of 120 days.
    - No. of RBCs is 4.5-5 million/cubic mm. of blood.
2. **White Blood Corpuscles (WBCS)**
    - Also called **leucocytes**, rounded, with a nucleus and far less numerous than RBCs (8,000 per cubic mm. of blood).
    - Manufactured in Red Bone marrow.
    - Act as the soldiers of body's defence system.
3. **Platelets**
    - Also called **thrombocytes** and are about 2,50,000 per cubic mm. of blood.
    - Manufactured in Red Bone marrow
    - Help the blood to clot.

BLOOD GROUPINGS

- Father of Blood Grouping : *Karl Landsteiner.*
- He discovered A, B and O blood groups.
- Decastello and Strurle discovered AB blood group.

Blood Group	Can donate to	Can receive from
A	A, AB	A, O
B	B, AB	B, O
AB	AB	A, B, AB, O
O	A, B, AB, O	O

RH FACTOR

- It is a blood antigen found in RBC.
- A person can be Rh+ or Rh– depending upon the presence of Rh factor in RBC.
- A very important point is Rh+ can receive blood from both Rh+ and Rh– but Rh– can receive blood from Rh– only.
- In world population, Rh+ are 85% and Rh– are 15%.
- Blood transfusion technique was developed by **James Blundell**.

NERVOUS SYSTEM

- The nerves, the brain and the spinal cord constitute the nervous system.
- Nervous system controls and regulates the activities of all the other systems of the body.

BRAIN

- Brain is the main organ of the nervous system. It consists of *cerebrum, cerebellum and medulla oblongata.*

Cerebrum

- It controls the voluntary actions and is the seat of intelligence.
- Its outer grey matter is the most important part.

Cerebellum

- It is concerned with equilibrium of the body and co-ordination of muscles.

Medulla Oblongata

- Lowest part of the brain and is connected with the spinal cord.
- It controls the involuntary actions.

BALANCED DIET

- *The components of food are :* Carbohydrates, Fats, Proteins, Minerals, Vitamins, Water and Roughage.
- If all the components are present in optimum proportions and quantity for maintaining the body in perfect state of health, activity and development then the food is called *balanced diet.*

CARBOHYDRATES

- *Constitutes 3 elements :* Carbon, Hydrogen and Oxygen.
- Daily requirement 500 gms. 1 gm gives 17 KJ of energy.
- The carbohydrates of the food eaten, after being processed in the alimentary canal and liver, are supplied to the tissues mainly as glucose, often called blood sugar.
- *Sources :* 3 main cereals (wheat, rice and maize), sugar cane, milk, fruits, honey, beet, etc.
- *They are of 3 types :* Cellulose, Starch and Sugar.
- *Structurally, carbohydrates are of 3 types :* Monosaccharides, Disaccharides and Polysaccharides.
- Excess carbohydrate is stored in the liver in the form of glycogen.

FATS

- Provides twice the energy of carbohydrates (1 gm provides 37 KJ of energy).
- Acts as the reserve food material because excess fat is stored in the liver and as adipose tissue.
- An enzyme called *Lipase* digests fats. It breaks down into fatty acids and glycerol.
- *Daily requirement*: 50 gms.

PROTEINS

- Made up of Carbon, Hydrogen, Oxygen and Nitrogen.
- Important for growth and repair of the body.
- Made up of amino acids.
- *Kwashiorkar* and *Marasmus* are the diseases which occur due to deficiency of protein.

MINERALS

MACRO ELEMENTS

Mineral Elements	Sources	Significance	Effect of deficiency
Calcium (Ca)#	Milk, cereals, cheese, green vegetables	Required for formation of teeth and bones, blood clothing, functions of nerves and muscles	Weak teeth and bones; retarded body growth
Phosphorus (P)	Milk, meat, cereals	Required for formation of teeth and bones and acid-base balance; component of ATP, DNA, RNA	Weak teeth and bones; retarded body growth and physiology
Sulphur (S)	Many proteins of food	Component of many amino acids	Disturbed protein metabolism
Potassium (K)	Meat, milk, cereals, fruits and vegetables	Required for acid-base balance, water regulation and function of nerves	Low blood pressure, weak muscles; risk of paralysis
Chlorine (Cl)	Table salt	Required for acid-base balance; component of gastric juice	Loss of appetite; muscle cramps
Sodium (Na)	Table salt	Required for acid base and water balance and nervous functions	Low blood pressure, Loss of appetite; muscle cramps
Magnesium (Mg)	Cereals, green vegetables	Cofactor of many enzymes of glycolysis and a number of other metabolic reactions dependent upon ATP	Irregularities of metabolism principally affecting nervous functions
Iron (Fe)	Meat, eggs, cereals, green vegetables	Component of haemoglobin and cytochromes	Anaemia, weakness and weak immunity
Iodine (I)	Milk, cheese, sea food, iodized salt	Important component of thyroxine hormone	Goitre, Cretinism

 # The salt of Ca required by our body is $Ca_3(PO_4)_2$

VITAMINS

Necessary for normal growth, good health, good vision, proper digestion of the body, etc. They do not provide energy to our body.

Vitamins can be divided into two categories :

(*i*) **Water-soluble :** Vitamin B-complex, Vitamin C.

(*ii*) **Fat-soluble :** Vitamin A, Vitamin D, Vitamin E, Vitamin K.

TYPE OF VITAMINS

Vitamin	Chemical Name	Properties	Deficiency Disease
A	Retinol	General health giving vitamin, can be stored in liver	Night blindness
B_1	Thiamine	For growth, carbo-hydrate metabolism, functioning of heart	Beri-Beri
B_2	Riboflavin	For keeping skin and mouth healthy	Cheilosis
B_5	Niacin	For healthy skin, sound mental health	Pellagra
B_6	Pyridoxine	Processing of proteins and for nervous system	Convulsions in child
B_{12}	Cynacobalamin	Required for formation and maturation of RBCs	Pernicious-anaemia
C	Ascorbic Acid	For keeping teeth, gums and joints healthy. Gets destroyed on heating	Scurvy
D	Calciferol	For normal bones and teeth, can be stored in liver	Rickets
E	Tocopherol	For normal reproduction, removes scars and wrinkles	Sterility
K	Phylloquinone	For normal clotting of blood	Haemophilia

WATER

Important in digestion, transportation, excretion and to regulate body temperature (body contains 65% water).

ROUGHAGE

- Fibrous material present in the cell wall of plants.
- Mainly contains cellulose.
- It doesn't provide energy but only helps in retaining water in the body.
- One of the common source is *Daliya*, which we eat in our homes.

HUMAN ENDOCRINE SYSTEM

Gland	Hormone	Functions
Hypothalamus	Releasing and inhibiting hormones and factors Posterior pituitary hormones produced here	Control of anterior pituitary hormones
Posterior pituitary gland	Receives hormones from hypothalamus-no hormones synthesized here Stores and secretes the following: Oxytocin Antidiuretic hormone (ADH) (vasopressin)	Ejection of milk from mammary gland, contraction of uterus during birth Reduction of urine secretion by kidney

Gland	Hormone	Functions
Thyroid gland	Triiodothyronine (T_3) and thyroxine (T_4) Calcitonin	Regulation of basal metabolic rate, growth and development Decreases blood calcium level
Adrenal cortex	Glucocorticoids (cortisol) Mineralocorticoids (aldosterone)	Protein breakdown glucose/ glycogen synthesis, adaptation to stress, anti-inflammatory/allergy effects Na^+ retention in kidney, Na^+ and K^+ ratios in extracellular and intracellular fluids, raises blood pressure
Adrenal medulla	Adrenaline (epinephrine) Noradrenaline (norepinephrine)	Increases rate and force of heartbeat, construction of skin and gut capillaries Dilation of arterioles of heart and skeletal muscles, raising blood glucose level General construction of small arteries, raising of blood pressure
Islets of Langerhans	Insulin (beta cells) Glucagon (alphacells)	Decreases blood glucose level, increases glucose and amino acid uptake and utilization by cells Increases blood glucose level, breakdown of glycogen to glucose in liver
Stomach	Gastrin	Secretion of gastric juices
Duodenum	Secretin Cholecystokinin (pancreozymin)	Secretion of pancreatic juice Inhibits gastric secretion Emptying of gall bladder and release of pancreatic juice into duodenum
Kidney	Renin	Conversion of angiotensinogen into angiotensin
Ovary	Oestrogens Progesterone	Female secondary sex characteristic, oestrous cycle Gestation, inhibition of ovulation

Gland	Hormone	Functions
Corpus luteum	Progesterone and oestrogen Progesterone and oestrogen	Growth and development of uterus Foetal development
Placenta	Chorionic gonadotrophin Human placental lactogen	Maintenance of corpus luteum Stimulates mammary growth
Testis	Testosterone	Male secondary sexual characteristics

■ ■

SPORTS

SUMMER OLYMPIC GAMES

Games	Year	Venue
I	1896	Athens (Greece)
II	1900	Paris (France)
III	1904	St. Louis (USA)
IV	1908	London (UK)
V	1912	Stockholm (Sweden)
VII	1920	Antwerp (Belgium)
VIII	1924	Paris (France)
IX	1928	Amsterdam (Netherlands)
X	1932	Los Angeles (USA)
XI	1936	Berlin (Germany)
XIV	1948	London (UK)
XV	1952	Helsinki (Finland)
XVI	1956	Melbourne (Australia)
XVII	1960	Rome (ltaly)
XVIII	1964	Tokyo (Japan)
XIX	1968	Mexico City (Mexico)
XX	1972	Munich (West Germany)
XXI	1976	Montreal (Canada)
XXII	1980	Moscow (Soviet Vnion)
XXIII	1984	Los Angeles (USA)
XXIV	1988	Seoul (South Korea)
XXV	1992	Barcelona (Spain)
XXVI	1996	Atlanta (USA)
XXVII	2000	Sydney (Australia)
XXVIII	2004	Athens (Greece)
XXIX	2008	Beijing (China)
XXX	2012	London (UK)
XXXI	2016	Rio de Janeiro (Brazil)
XXXII	2020	Japan

Note :
- Olympic Games could not take place in 1916 due to World War I.
- Olympic Games could not take place in 1940 and 1944 due to World War II.
- 31st Olympic Games of 2016 will be held for the first time in South America.

ASIAN GAMES UPDATE

Year	Games	Host City	Country
1951	I	New Delhi	India
1954	II	Manila	Philippines
1958	III	Tokyo	Japan
1962	IV	Jakarta	Indonesia
1966	V	Bangkok	Thailand
1970	VI	Bangkok	Thailand
1974	VII	Tehran	Iran
1978	VIII	Bangkok	Thailand
1982	IX	New Delhi	India
1986	X	Seoul	South Korea
1990	XI	Beijing	China
1994	XII	Hiroshima	Japan
1998	XIII	Bangkok	Thailand
2002	XIV	Busan	South Korea
2006	XV	Doha	Qatar
2010	XVI	Guangzhou	China
2014	XVII	Incheon	South Korea
2018	XVIII	Jakarta	Indonesia

COMMONWEALTH GAMES

Year	Games	Host City	Country
1930	I	Hamilton	Canada
1934	II	London	UK
1938	III	Sydeny	Australia
1950	IV	Auckland	New Zealand
1954	V	Vancouver	Canada
1958	VI	Cardiff	UK
1962	VII	Perth	Australia
1966	VIII	Kingston	Jamaica
1970	IX	Edinburgh	UK
1974	X	Christchurch	New Zealand
1978	XI	Edmonton	Canada

Year	Games	Host City	Country
1982	XII	Brisbane	Australia
1986	XIII	Edinburgh	UK
1990	XIV	Auckland	New Zealand
1994	XV	Victoria	Canada
1998	XVI	Kuala Lumpur	Malaysia

Year	Games	Host City	Country
2002	XVII	Manchester	UK
2006	XVIII	Melbourne	Australia
2010	XIX	New Delhi	India
2014	XX	Glasgow	Scotland (UK)
2018	XXI	Gold Coast	Australia
2022	XXII	Durban	South Africa

FOOTBALL WORLD CUP WINNERS

Year	Host	Winner	Runners-up
1930	Uruguay	Uruguay	Argentina
1934	Italy	Italy	Czechoslovakia
1938	France	Italy	Hungary
1950	Brazil	Uruguay	Brazil
1954	Switzerland	West Germany	Hungary
1958	Sweden	Brazil	Sweden
1962	Chile	Brazil	Czechoslovakia
1966	England	England	West Germany
1970	Mexico	Brazil	Italy
1974	West Germany	West Germany	Netherlands
1978	Argentina	Argentina	Netherlands
1982	Spain	Italy	West Germany
1986	Mexico	Argentina	West Germany
1990	Italy	West Germany	Argentina
1994	USA	Brazil	Italy
1998	France	France	Brazil
2002	S. Korea/Japan	Brazil	Germany
2006	Germany	Italy	France
2010	South Africa	Spain	Netherlands
2014	Brazil	Germany	Argentina
2018	Russia	—	—
2022	Qatar	—	—

HOCKEY WORLD CUP WINNERS

Year	Host	Winner	Runner-up
1971	Barcelona, Spain	Pakistan	Spain
1973	Amstelveen, Netherlands	Netherlands	India
1975	Kuala Lumpur, Malaysia	India	Pakistan
1978	Buenos Aires, Argentina	Pakistan	Netherlands
1982	Mumbai, India	Pakistan	West Germany
1986	London, England	Australia	England

Year	Host	Winner	Runner-up
1990	Lahore (Pakistan)	Netherlands	Pakistan
1994	Sydney, Australia	Pakistan	Netherlands
1998	Utrecht, Netherlands	Netherlands	Spain
2002	Kuala Lumpur, Malaysia	Germany	Australia
2006	Monchengladbach, Germany	Germany	Australia
2010	New Delhi, India	Australia	Germany
2014	The Haque, Netherlands	—	—
2018	Bhubaneswar, India	—	—

ORGANIZATION AND RESULTS OF THE WORLD CUPS

Year	Host Nation (s)	Final Venue	Winner	Runner-up
1975	England	Lord's, London	West Indies	Australia
1979	England	Lord's, London	West Indies	England
1983	England	Lord's, London	India	West Indies
1987	India/Pakistan	Eden Gardens, Kolkata	Australia	England
1992	Australia/New Zealand	MCG, Melbourne	Pakistan	England
1996	India/Pakistan/Sri Lanka	Gaddafi Stadium, Lahore	Sri Lanka	Australia
1999	England	Lord's London	Australia	Pakistan
2003	South Africa	Wanderers, Johannesbury	Australia	India
2007	West Indies	Kensington Oval, Bridgetown	Australia	Sri Lanka
2011	Bangladesh/India/ Sri Lanka	Wankhede Stadium, Mumbai	India	Sri Lanka
2015	Australia/ New Zealand	Melbourne, Australia	Australia	New Zealand
2019	England			

PLAYER OF THE TOURNAMENT IN WORLD CUP CRICKET

Year	Player	Performance Details
1996	Sanath Jayasuriya	221 runs and 7 wickets
1999	Lance Klusener	281 runs and 17 wickets
2003	Sachin Tendulkar	673 runs and 2 wickets
2007	Glenn McGrath	26 wickets
2011	Yuvraj Singh	362 runs and 15 wickets
2015	Mitchell Starc	22 wickets in 8 matches

FAMOUS CUPS AND TROPHIES

Sport	Cups and Trophies
Cricket	The Ashes, Anthony Demellow Trophy, C.K. Naidu Trophy, Cooch-Behar Trophy, Deodhar Trophy, Duleep Trophy, lrani Trophy, Moin-ud-dowla-Cup, Natwest Trophy, Ranji Trophy, Rohinton Bria Trophy, Sheesh Mahal Trophy, Sheffield Shield
Foot Ball	B.C. Roy Trophy, Bordoloi Trophy, DCM Cup, Durand Cup, G.V. Raja Memorial Trophy Mardeka Cup, Nehru Gold Cup, Rovers Cup, Santosh Trophy

Sport	Cups and Trophies
Golf	Canada Cup, Muthiah Gold Cup, Ryder Cup, Walker Cup
Hockey	Agha Khan Cup, Azlan Shah Cup, Beighten Cup, Dhyan Chand Trophy, Gyanvati Devi Trophy, Indira Gandhi Gold Cup, Khan Abdul Gaffar Cup, Lady Ratna Tata Cup (women), Modi Gold Cup, Murugappa Gold Cup, Obaidullah Gold Cup, Rangaswami Cup
Table Tennis	Corbillion Cup (women), Jayalaxmi, Cup(wamen), Swaythling Cup (men), U. Thant Cup
Lawn Tennis	Davis Cup, Hamlet Cup, Gaffar, Cup, Australian open, French Open, Wimbledon, US Open
Badminton	Ibrahim Rahimatullah Challenge Cup, Thomas Cup (men), Uber Cup (women), Narang Cup
Boxing	Aspy Adjahia Trophy
Rowing	Wellington Trophy
Bridge	Ruia Trophy
Polo	Ezat Cup, Winchester Cup
Chess	Khaitan Trophy

NUMBER OF PLAYERS IN VARIOUS GAMES

Game	Number of Players
Baseball	9
Basketball	5
Cricket	11
Croquest	13 or 15
Football	11
Rugby Football	15

Game	Number of Players
Hockey	11
Lacrosse	12
Polo	4
Volleyball	6
Water polo	7
Netball	7

FAMOUS INDIAN SPORTSPERSONS

Sport	Sportspersons
Archery	Dola Banerjee, Jayant Talukdar, Limba Ram, Satyadev Prasad, Tarundeep Rai, Mangal Singh Champia, Bombayla Devi, Reena Kumari, Majhi Sawaiyan, Pranitha Vardhineni
Athletics	Anju Bobby George, Jyotirmoyee sikdar, Milkha Singh, Norman pritchard, P.T. Usha, T.C. Yohannan, Ashwini Nachappa
Badminton	Aparna Popat, Prakash Padukone, Pullela Gopichand, Anup Sridhar, Chetan Anand, Jwala Gutta, Saina Nehwal, Aparna Balan, Dipankar Bhattacharjee, Valiyaveetil Diju
Billiards	Pankaj Advani, Ashok shandilya, Michael Ferreira, Geet Sethi,Wilson Jones, Yasin Merchant
Boxing	Dingko Singh, Hawa Singh, Mohd. Ali Qamar, Vijender Singh, Akhil Kumar, Nanao Singh Thockchom, M.C. Mary Kom

Sport	Sportspersons
Chess	Dibyendu Barua, Koneru Humpy, Krishnan Sasikiran, Manuel Aaron, Parimarjan Negi, P.Harikrishna, Viswanathan Anand, Surya Shekhar Ganguly, Sahaj Grover, Abhijeet Gupta, D. Harika, Abhijeet Kunte, Tania Sachdev, Hetul Shah, S. Vijayalakshmi
Golf	Ali Sher, Arjun Atwal, Gaurav Ghei, Jeev Milkha Singh, Jyoti Randhawa, Shiv Kapur, Gaganjeet Bhullar, Shiv Chourasia
Hockey	Ajit Pal Singh, Balbir Singh Sr., Dhanraj Pillay, Dhyan Chand, Gagan Ajit Singh, K.D. Singh Babu, Leslie Claudius, Mohammed Shahid, Udham singh, Suman Bala
Shooting	Abhinav Bindra, Anjali Bhagwat, Jaspal Rana, Dr. Karni Singh, Rajyavardhan Singh Rathore, Randhir Singh, Samresh Jung, Tejaswini Sawant, Ronak Pandit, Manavjit Singh Sandhu, Pemba Tamang
Swimming	Bula Chowdhury, Khazan Singh, Mihir Sen, Rehan Poncha, Nafisa Ali, Sebastian Xavier, Nisha Millet, Aditya Raut, Arti Saha, Sachet Engineer
Table Tennis	Achanta Sharath Kamal, Chetan Baboor, Kamlesh Mehta, S. Raman
Tennis	Leander Paes, Mahesh Bhupathi, Ramanathan Krishnan, Ramesh Krishnan, Sania Mirza, Vijay Amritraj, Yuki Bhambri, Rohan Bopanna, Harsh Mankad, Nirupama Vaidyanathan
Football	Baichung Bhutia, Chuni Goswami, Jarnail Singh, Peter Thangaraj, P.K. Banerjee, Sailen Manna, I.M. Vijayan, Climax Lawrence, Gostha Pal, Mahesh Gawli, Shanmugam Venkatesh, Sunil Chetri

IMPORTANT SPORT TERMS

Sport	Terms
Basketball	Dunk, front court, held ball, lay up, pivot, rebound, steal
Billiards	Pot, Jigger, Pockets, bridge, hazard, jenney, cannons
Boxing	Jab, laying on knock, seconds out habbit punch, upper cut
Bridge	Dealer, dummy, revoke, tricks, little slam, four hearts
Badminton	Loab, let, drive, drop, love
Baseball	Balk, battery, diamond, catcher, fly outs, hit and run play pup outs, pitcher
Chess	Castle, diagonals, files, pawns pieces, promote, gambit, pawn
Cricket	Bye, draw, googly, topspin, over throw, duck, hit wicket
Football	Bend, dribble, dissent, dummy, feint, free kick, header, red card, throwins
Golf	Birdie, bogey, lie, tee, rough
Hockey	Bully, striking circle, pass back

NATIONAL GAMES OF SOME COUNTRIES

Game	Sports/Games
India	Hockey
Sri Lanka	Volleyball
USA	Baseball
Canada	Ice Hockey
Russia	Chess
England	Cricket and Rugby
Australia	Cricket
Malaysia	Badminton
Japan	Ju Jitsu
Spain	Bull Fighting

Game	Sports/Games
Brazil	Football
China	Table Tennis
Scotland	Rugby Football
Bhutan	Archery
Argentina	Pato
Bangladesh	Kabaddi
Pakistan	Hockey
France	Football
Indonsia	Badminton
Cuba	Baseball

RAJIV GANDHI KHEL RATNA AWARDEES

SL.	Year	Name of the Sportsperson(s)	Sport Discipline
1.	1991-92	Viswanathan Anand	Chess
2.	1992-93	Geet Sethi	Billiards
3.	1993-94	Not Conferred*	———
4.	1994-95	Cdr. Homi D. Motivala and Lt. Cdr. P.K.Garg	Yachting (team Event)
5.	1995-96	Karnam Malleswari	Weightlifting
6.	1996-97	Leander Paes and Nameirakpam Kunjarani (Joint)	Tennis and Weightlifting respectively
7.	1997-98	Sachin Tendulkar	Cricket
8.	1998-99	Jyotirmoyee Sikdar	Athletics
9.	1999-2000	Dhanraj Pillay	Hockey
10.	2000-01	Pullela Gopichand	Badminton
11.	2001-02	Abhinav Bindra	Shooting
12.	2002-03	Anjali Ved Pathak Bhagwat and K.M. Beenamol (Joint)	Shooting and Athletics respectively
13.	2003-04	Anju Bobby George	Athletics
14.	2004-05	Rajyavardhan Singh Rathore	Shooting
15.	2005-06	Pankaj Advani	Billiards and Snooker
16.	2006-07	Manavjit Singh Sandhu	Shooting
17.	2007-08	Mahendra Singh Dhoni	Cricket
18.	2008-09	M.C. Mary Kom, Sushil Kumar and Vijendar Kumar	Boxing, Wrestling and Boxing respectively
19.	2009-10	Saina Nehwal	Badminton
20.	2010-11	Gagan Narang	Shooting
21.	2011-12	Vijay kumar and Yogeshwar Dutt	Shooting and Wrestling
22.	2012-13	Ronjan Sodhi	Shooting
23.	2013-14	Not Conferred*	———
24.	2014-15	Sania Mirza	Tennis
25.	2015-16	P. V. Sindhu, Deepa Kamikar, Sakshi Bhai and Jitu Rai	Badminton, Gymnastics, Wrestling, Shooting
26.	2016-2017	Devendra Jhajaria, Sardar Singh	Javelin throw, Hockey

*The award was not conferred upon any sportsperson or team in the year 1993-94 & 2013-14.

■■

9 789387 766358

Printed by Libri Plureos GmbH in Hamburg, Germany